Michael/Frank

MICHAEL/FRANK

Studies on Frank O'Connor

edited by Maurice Sheehy

Alfred A. Knopf *New York 1969*

THIS IS A BORZOI BOOK
PUBLISHED BY ALFRED A. KNOPF, INC.

American
First Edition

Published in the United States by Alfred A. Knopf, Inc., New York.
Distributed by Random House, Inc., New York.
Originally published in Great Britain by Macmillan and Co. Ltd.,
London.

Library of Congress Catalog Card Number: 69-19171

Manufactured in Great Britain

Contents

Foreword

Frank O'Connor had two names and lived a life with many facets. Yet everything that he did, however unexpected or even contradictory it might seem, was informed by the same single-minded and passionate integrity. The young Irish rebel and the mature wartime friend of Britain, the eccentric librarian, the enthusiastic man of the theatre and the meticulous self-taught scholar, the sonorous translator of Irish poetry and the superlative short-story writer, the inspiring public lecturer and the dogged master of the seminar – all were unquestionably the same unique and original man.

Frank O'Connor died on 10 March 1966. He was then in his early sixties at the height of his powers as a writer and an authority on many aspects of Irish literature. His death has brought a grievous loss, not only to those who knew him, but also to countless readers and pupils who have been robbed of what he had still to write in his books and to say in his lectures. It has also broken one of the last links with those great figures of the Irish Renaissance, Yeats, AE, James Stephens and Sean O'Casey, all of whom were published by my firm, and who were personal friends of myself and my family.

I cannot claim to have known him well, yet by O'Connor's own account I may once have exerted a useful influence on his life. When he was trying to be a librarian, run a theatre and write, all at the same time, I said to him, 'You've reached the stage where you must decide whether you're going to be a good writer or a good public servant. You can't be both.' This is not a proposition to which I would give universal application, but it was manifestly true in O'Connor's case, and I think he knew it. Probably I did no more than give him a push in the direction in which he had already decided to go, a service authors often require of their publishers. If I was able to help him on his way, I am very glad to have done so.

Eighteen of his friends and colleagues, who knew him far better than I did, have come together in this volume not to bury or to praise, but to attempt some assessment of his qualities as a writer and to set down their vivid and varied impressions of the man as he was. This book may thus complement – though it cannot, alas, complete – the inimitable picture that he has given in the two volumes of his unfinished autobiography.

Harold Macmillan

King of the Castle

HONOR TRACY

For me, Frank O'Connor always was and always will be Michael O'Donovan. Why, with such a beautiful name, he had to bestow on himself that mongrel appellation I never understood. And a real Michael he was, brave, chivalrous, vehement, with sword ever sharp and ready for a dragon sufficiently misguided to cross his path.

His nose for a dragon was quite remarkably keen. One of my earliest, fondest recollections is of the warm rich voice denouncing poor harmless old Lennox Robinson. 'That man is EVIL!' it declared, with profound conviction: 'the embodiment of EVIL!' Apparently, long ago, they had disagreed over something to do with the Abbey Theatre.

Quite often, too, it happened that people he had loved and admired turned out to be dragons after all: or, rather, turned into dragons, for otherwise he must have been mistaken about them to begin with, the very idea of which was absurd. Thus, after a separation, it was advisable to go warily when inquiring for his cronies, lest one or more should meanwhile have undergone this metamorphosis.

It was always a secret terror of mine that one day I also should wake to find myself a dragon. Somehow or other I never did, even in the hazardous Roger Casement period. Michael then was unable to think or speak for any length of time about anything else, and, as always, he expected his friends to be in full agreement with him. Since he knew for a fact that the diaries were forged, there was no room for discussion. Dissenters were either perverse or misguidedly, pigheadedly, loyal to England.

It was natural that he should find my own attitude peculiarly exasperating. I did not, could not, believe in the forgeries, but fervently wished that I could. The idea of all those stuffy civil servants diligently setting about their nefarious work entranced me. One day, as he was haranguing me, I imprudently begged him to help my unbelief with a little concrete evidence.

'Honor, me love,' he roared, 'you're talking like a blo'dy Englishwoman.'

But he even forgave me for that in time.

His flair for detecting evil in improbable places was counterbalanced by one for discovering extraordinary merits in the most ordinary – to use no stronger term – people one could hope to find. Many of them are still alive, or at least as alive as they ever were, so that we must not explore the matter too fully. But he had gathered a notable collection of them over the years. It was touching how he would quote their remarks and uphold their opinions, much as Stendhal did those of the Comte de Tracy, and how he would press their letters on us to read. Those of a certain American professor I shall never forget: they were usually concerned with his dreams, which he described in the lavish transatlantic way, pouring out three hundred words where thirty would have been excessive, and which were so utterly prosaic and uneventful that he might just as well have stayed awake.

This endearing characteristic of Michael's puzzled me at first, but I think the explanation was simple enough. He did not want any other lions knocking about in the vicinity. He had to be king of the castle, but, to make up for it, he freely showered titles and Orders on his entourage. Once this was done, he had no difficulty in persuading himself that it was deserved.

He was an extremely kind and generous man and, like many Irish people, particularly so to those in trouble. He was always giving – his time, his sympathy, his knowledge, his money. One day, as we were chuckling over a lawsuit I was about to bring, very amusing in itself but apt to be tiresome if it failed, he suddenly, in the most casual tone, said, 'I've fifteen hundred dollars coming that you could have.' He meant it, too, and he was never rich. Nothing was too much for a friend, just as nothing was too bad for an enemy – in theory, that is, for I never heard of his doing anyone harm. But he had a good Irish memory, and whenever certain names were mentioned there would be a glorious burst of invective: once he really quarrelled that was the end, and no one got a second chance.

It was not merely anger and grief of his own that stayed with him. He could be just as implacable about the wrongs of others. The first time we ever met, in 1946, he told me with passionate indignation the story of the Tailor and Ansty, his wife, of the merry old countryman with his fund of spicy tales, of the author who collected and innocently published them, of the *furor hibernicus* that followed, of the banning of the book and its public burning by a local priest, the shunning of the pair by the neighbours, the broken-hearted Tailor's death and Ansty's lonely ending in the workhouse: a story in every way typical of the 'Holy Ireland' that Michael detested and that to the end of his days he could never repeat but the rage welled up in him anew.

In many ways he was as Irish as could be, but he had a seriousness rarely found in that mercurial race. He meant what he said, and he had no patience with humbug. People were always attacking him from no real conviction but because it was the correct thing to do, and this revolted him. He amazed me once by his fury at some poor hack who had been squirting venom over him in a government propaganda-sheet that no rational person would think of reading anyhow. He explained, however, that he did not care in the least what the scribbler wrote. It was just that shortly afterwards the little chap had accosted him with a beaming smile and the words, 'Ah, Mr O'Connor, I believe we were crossing swords?' The next moment there was a rumble of laughter: 'Yeats was the one for fellows like that! He never remembered their names.'

Now and again he shook the dust of Ireland off his feet for ever. Presently we would hear with joy, but no surprise, that he was back. He had love affairs with England and America and brief flirtations with the Continent, but to Ireland he was fatally and indissolubly married, deny it as he would.

He had various other illusions about himself, some delightfully comic. More than once he assured me that he had missed his vocation and ought to have been a priest. One often hears such things from Irishmen in their cups; but Michael was dead sober and so plainly in earnest that, even if the vision of him celibate and caged in ecclesiastical discipline had not struck me dumb, I should not have dared to argue.

Undoubtedly he had a sense of frustration in his middle years, due perhaps to his gifts being greater than the scope they found. A writer of his talent required something bigger and grander than republican Ireland. That he felt this he seemed to show by the constant rewriting of work done long before, by the withdrawal into Gaelic mists, the obsessions and wrangles and hobby-horses. But towards the end he found a new and happy outlet in the lectures at Trinity College, into which, ill and tired as he often was, he put his whole heart.

That association with Trinity meant a great deal to him. I well remember the scene when he got his doctorate *honoris causa* there. Apparelled in hired formal dress and academic robes, walking in dignity up the aisle to the platform with the other luminaries, he looked strangely unlike his bohemian self. As he went by he gave me a broad wink and a sardonic grin, which didn't fool me for a moment. This was one of the good days of his life.

Michael O'Donovan's Wild Son

SEAN HENDRICK

June 1921 was a month of glorious sunshine, but neither I nor anybody else in Cork could enjoy it. The heart of the city was in ruins, the City Hall and Public Library were burnt-out shells and the long nights were raucous with the rattle of rifle and machine-gun fire. Curfew was in force and everyone had to be indoors from five o'clock in the afternoon – everyone, that is, except the British forces, military, auxiliaries and black-and-tans. But for the tension and excitement of the times it would have been depressing to watch each golden day go uselessly by. In July came the Truce and we could breathe freely again and walk our streets in peace. It was then that I met Michael for the first time and started a friendship that was to last until his death.

He was eighteen years old, three years my junior. We got on well together although, or perhaps because, we were totally unlike in temperament. We had certain interests in common, cultural and national, and these we argued about endlessly. Michael had a fantastic memory. Having no money with which to buy books or periodicals he copied out and memorized whatever appealed to him, largely poetry, and was able to cover any argument at the drop of a hat with a quotation from his built-in library. This was often annoying, but there was little I could do about it, and usually while we started from the same port, as it were, his memory and imagination would sweep us all over the seven seas, finally arriving at a harbour where we had never expected to drop anchor. Even so the trip was never less than exhilarating.

In appearance he was tall and bony, almost gaunt, and his habit of pulling forward his shoulders made him look almost concave about the chest. He had never played games, while I had played every game that came my way. He used to wear a homespun jacket that hung from him almost as if it were on a peg and altogether he looked rather like a young Russian peasant. 'It's due to all that Russian literature you are reading,' said Corkery to him one day as we sat on a grassy ditch in the sun.

Michael's neighbours in Harrington Square and Dillon's Cross, mostly people almost as poor as himself, liked him, but were quite sure from their own hard experience of life that any young fellow who could not hold down a job, even as a messenger boy, would never come to anything.

Our friend Daniel Corkery suggested to us that we form a debating society. There was no need. The Ireland of the time was one big debating society. Following the Truce, negotiations for a settlement had started. In the heady atmosphere of the time it never occurred to me or, I think, to Michael that our side might be forced to accept anything less than what it was looking for, so we were mad as hatters when the text of the Anglo-Irish Treaty was published in December. We heard the news standing in a crowd that had gathered outside the *Cork Examiner* awaiting the result of the crucial Dail vote – 64 for, 57 against – and the narrowness of the margin was no comfort.

The next few months were hectic. If before the Treaty was passed it had been debate, after its passing it was passion, bitterness and invective that filled the air. On 22 February 1922 the Ard Fheis was held in the Mansion House in Dublin and Michael and I attended as delegates, which we were not, but two I.R.A. officers who were too busy with army affairs gave us their admission tickets and voting instructions. If the Treaty was to be put to a vote, we were to reject it. That suited us. But in the event no vote was taken on this issue. All the leaders were on the platform, and there must have been over two thousand delegates present. It was a stormy meeting, but while inflammatory speeches were made on both sides the general feeling seemed to be to avoid a split at all costs. So Michael and I returned to Cork in the same frame of mind as we had set out and very little wiser.

Fortunately, apart from settling the affairs of the nation to our own satisfaction, we had other interests. Daniel Corkery lived in our neighbourhood, and his house was a refuge from acrimony. Beethoven, Mozart, Bach and other composers played on his big cabinet gramophone were a welcome change, as were our discussions on literature and events in the world at large. Twenty or more years our senior, Corkery was one of the gentlest of men, so much so that few suspected the fierce and angry spirit which his manner concealed. He was an excellent painter in his favourite medium, water-colours, and we had many outings with him on his sketching trips.

But outside this pleasant, relaxed little world events were building up to a climax. Meetings and counter-meetings and passionate oratory kept the cauldron boiling. Although the 1st Southern Division of the I.R.A., of which the Cork Brigades formed part, was firmly anti-Treaty, there was plenty of support for the settlement among the people in the area as a whole. But in the circumstances of the time, not unnaturally, it was rather subdued, a bit timid and confused. Coming away from one of these public meetings one might, as Michael and I mixed with the dispersing crowds, we saw a woman in a shawl pulling along in front of us a small boy about six years old with a little tricolour on top of a short stick in his hand. He was out when he should have been in bed; there were crowds and bands and speeches and cheering. The excitement was too much for him. 'Up Michael Collins,' he piped at the top of his voice as he waved his little flag frantically in the air. 'Sh-sh, Johnny, sh-sh!' said the woman, looking anxiously about her. Johnny was dumbfounded. There was a moment of silence and then: 'Is it *down* Michael Collins so-o-o ma-a-a?' dragging out his vowels in the sing-song Cork fashion. But like the rest of the nation the poor woman had no answer to that one.

On 28 June the Four Courts was attacked and the Civil War was on. Michael and I went to the local headquarters at Union Quay and volunteered our services. We were posted to publicity, and if it was not what we would have chosen it was probably the only place where he would not have been in the way. Michael especially was very disappointed, and the sight of Sean O'Faolain with a rifle on his shoulder, riding through town on a lorry, made him really mad. O'Faolain had been a frequent visitor to Corkery's house and had shared our talk and our music.

Our first job in publicity was to act as censors of the *Cork Examiner*, our local daily, which was strongly pro-Treaty. Our immediate boss was Liam Manahan, a very lively, good-humoured Limerick man who knew far more about the personalities and inner workings of the movement than we did. Later, when our army was trying – unsuccessfully – to hold positions on a front stretching from Limerick to Waterford, Erskine Childers arrived in Cork and directed publicity, and we worked with him from that time forward. He and Michael became our correspondents in the fighting zone, and Michael on his first assignment distinguished himself by wandering into the enemy lines around Kilmallock and being captured. For some hours he was held prisoner in a farmhouse which in turn was attacked by anti-Treaty forces and surrendered after a sharp fight. So the farmhouse was captured and Michael recaptured before the day was out.

In the *Cork Examiner* offices life was less exciting. As censors we were, I think, a dead loss. Michael and I knew nothing whatever about the running of a newspaper, and as I can see now in retrospect the staff had very little trouble in frustrating our endeavours at every turn. But at least we were busy if ineffective. The personal feelings of the employees never cost us a thought. Even that they might have ideas of their own about what we were doing was only brought home to us the day we clashed with their chief reporter, a neighbour of our own. Michael and I were working away happily in a room where files of the *Cork Examiner* were kept. We had scissors and paste and a large scrapbook and were cutting up the files to get material for our publicity. Our principal sources were the speeches of our opponents with which we hoped to damn them out of their own mouths by using things they had said a week or a month or a year before. Then the door opened and — the chief reporter stood there with his hand on the knob and horror in his eyes. He took one, long shocked look at our activities, swore an almighty, full-blooded oath and retreated, slamming the door behind him. The office saw no more of him that day and we heard afterwards that he had fled to the nearest pub and got mouldy drunk.

An Only Child sketches in the rest of our time in publicity – the evacuation of Cork, the fortunes of our printing press in the west and our subsequent return to the city. Here, in November, only a couple of days before the judicial murder of Erskine Childers, I was picked up and put in the Female Gaol until January 1923 when I was transferred to the internment camp at Newbridge. In April Michael was arrested and sent to Gormanstown Camp. From the time of my imprisonment a whole year was to go by before I saw Michael again.

It was a year that had affected him profoundly.

After his release from Gormanstown Michael took no further active part in the politics of the time. The writer in him took over and stayed firmly in the saddle thereafter. At first it was mainly poetry and the poets. Browning, Whitman, Hopkins and a dozen others were gutted and quoted in our rambles whenever the scene or the occasion made them seem relevant. Even poor verse sounded good when rolled out in Michael's rich, bass voice:

> *I have been faithful to thee, Cynara! in my fashion,*
> *Flung roses, roses, riotously with the throng.*
> *Striving to put thy pale lost lilies out of mind*
> *But I was desolate and sick of an old passion . . .*

To hear him recite this was to experience a pleasure altogether disproportionate to the merit of poor Dowson's self-pitying lines. He made them sound almost like poetry. Even after more than

B

forty years I can still remember one magical night as we came
from the Opera House and were crossing Patrick's Bridge,
beneath us the river lanterned with lupin-lights and overhead the
flash of a seagull's wings in the dark. We walked slowly and in
silence until Michael, head thrown back, recited almost to himself: 'Gondolas, lights and music drunkenly swam in the shimmer-
ing air.' But whether he was repeating something he had read or
just improvising I never knew. It was not a moment for the
intrusion of that kind of curiosity.

From the time I first met him Michael's chief and almost only
ambition was to become a poet, and hardly a day went by without
a poem or two being turned out by him, and indeed for some
years from 1924 onwards it remained poetry, either original or
translations from the Irish poets. In Gormanstown, as he himself
tells us, he had discovered grammar, and indeed for some weeks
after his release he nearly drove me mad in his preoccupation with
it. Day after day when I called to his house I would find him in a
blaze of enthusiasm over the obscurities of grammar and syntax,
subjects which I found incredibly boring, but which he found
thereafter invaluable in his translations of Irish poetry. At this
time, too, he was finding an outlet for his work in the columns of
the *Irish Statesman* to which he continued to contribute until that
journal ceased publication in 1930. From now on living became a
little easier for him. As well as the odd cheque from the *Irish
Statesman* he had now secured a job as County Librarian for Cork,
after having served some time in the county libraries of Sligo and
Wicklow, and in 1927 he went on a short trip to Paris. There he
called upon Joyce, and while I gathered they had got on pretty
well together I think on the whole it was rather a disappointing
meeting. Instead of traversing the landscape of literature, as
Michael had anticipated, Joyce was much more interested in finding out if certain colloquial words and phrases were still current
in Cork. For example, did the people there still say, when they
wanted you to look at something, 'Have a dake (d'fheach?) at
that' or 'Take a scance at that'? It is interesting to find Joyce

writing in a letter to Harriet Weaver that same year: 'A young man called on me before I left Paris, knew a lot of it [*Work In Progress*?] by heart, recites it to his friends and was very enthusiastic. I found he did not understand many of the words.' It could have been Michael.

From this trip Michael brought back two things with him, a copy of *Pomes Penyeach* for me and for himself a huge, round black hat of the kind popularly associated with artists – or Sandeman's Port – which he wore through the streets of Cork to my great embarrassment.

Michael was twenty-one when he was released from the internment camp at Gormanstown, and I think his mother's remark when he arrived home had a lot of truth in it. 'It made a man of you,' she said. He had now accumulated experiences not to be found, as heretofore, between the covers of books, but in his judgments he was almost as unpredictable as ever. When Kevin O'Higgins was assassinated in 1927 I called on Michael one evening and found he had cut a large picture of O'Higgins from one of the daily papers and pinned it up on the wall of his room. When I asked him why, he vigorously defended the gesture, but a few days later the picture was taken down and never referred to again. Pedestalled; reconsidered; toppled. Ah, well! with Michael it had even happened to Shakespeare, about whom he had a flaring row a few years later with a young poet, John Lane of Carrigaline, Co. Cork, who in his teens had sent Michael some of his poetry which we found most extraordinary for a lad of sixteen or seventeen, both in its themes and the language in which it was written. Quite recently I had a letter from Lane telling me about the row with Michael. He writes: 'One day somebody told me how "my friend, Frank O'Connor" had attacked Shakespeare in some paper or other. It seemed more than I could believe. How could anybody belittle this messiah of our literature? When we met again I told him what I had heard and also that I did not agree with him on the matter. A flare-up followed in which I was overcome for want of words. He got very annoyed and, strangely

enough, somewhat personal. I then indicated that I was going to
have no more to do with him and left the room in a huff . . . Next
time and I think the last time I saw him was at Shannonpark Cross
near here. He was on his way to Crosshaven on a bike. It was
summertime. He stopped to have a chat with me. We talked
about writing. He said that he was just beginning to feel that he
was "able to write at last". He also said that "at about forty we
will begin to think we are able to write for the first time". He
was then writing a short story about his first confession, he said.
After a while we parted and he continued his cycle ride to Crosshaven.'

But if young Lane had been more mature or had known
Michael better he would have understood what happened to
Shakespeare. He would have known that Michael's approach to
the great was to see them without any of the trappings in which
time and tradition had clothed them. Strangers often found this
irreverence shocking. Indeed the 'certain resentful air of bragga-
docio' which he attributed to the young Shakespeare might be
applied also to the young O'Donovan. I remember listening in
one Sunday morning to 'The Critics' on the B.B.C. Michael was
one of the panel and the subject being discussed was a film on
Rembrandt which had just been released. After several of the
speakers had waffled about this and things seemed to be grinding
to a halt, the chairman called on Michael. Michael obliged
venomously: 'I don't understand all this talk about Rembrandt.
After all, what was he but an inspired doodler?' – savagely spitting
out the last two words.

In the seconds of shocked silence that followed I chuckled with
delight, for I knew it was not Rembrandt that was being attacked,
but the 'polite, meaningless words' of the other speakers. It was
not what Michael said in this case that mattered, but why he said
it – something that I had long since been accustomed to.

Since his schooldays the greatest influence in Michael's life had
been his old teacher, Daniel Corkery. It was Corkery who had
introduced him to and enthused about the Irish language. It was

Corkery who, in the field of ideas, had tilled the ground and ferti-
lised it for him. In such circumstances it was almost inevitable that
Michael, with his heart set on being a writer, should find himself
in a dilemma: in which language should he write, Irish or English?
I remember, when we discussed this problem and his mind was
still struggling with it, he handed me one day the first draft of his
poem 'Quest of Dead O'Donovans' with its unresolved ending:

> Beside that tomb his choice was made,
> And many a time unmade before
> The loneliness of these, his kin,
> Took up its dwelling in his mind.
>
> He stood on the last ledge of rock,
> And did not turn, as though he feared
> The desolation, or knew not
> Which side lay Ireland, which the sea.

Now, since the foundation of Corkery's philosophy was this
question of the Irish language, it was inevitable that a rift should
open between them when Michael's creative work was done
in English. But even apart from this, no artist I suppose can be
fully content with another man's vision of life, and as Michael's
need to assert himself became greater the old teacher–pupil
relationship disappeared. At the time when the bonds were
slackening Michael would say to me occasionally, with the glint
of battle in his eye: 'Corkery, ah! yes. A great little talent.' And if
the challenge went unheeded it was simply because it seemed
foolish to seek to diminish either by standing on the shoulders of
the other. Besides, I was accustomed by then to the fluctuations in
stature of Michael's gods. But whatever he might think of
Corkery the philosopher he retained to the end an immense
affection for Corkery the man.

Among the people we had met in Corkery's house was
Lennox Robinson. He it was who was responsible for getting
Michael into the County Library service and who, when we were
planning the setting up of a drama group towards the end of the

'twenties, offered us his play *The Round Table*, free of royalties, for our first production. This was a welcome gesture as while we had plenty of ideas as to what we wanted to do, we had no money to do it. Michael was to be in charge of production and I was to be stage-manager. That Michael knew nothing about producing plays and I knew nothing about stage-managing them did not trouble us at all. We both agreed that our drama group could not be run by a committee. The producer was to be given a free hand in the choice of both plays and cast and members were bound to accept the parts allotted them. There were to be no stars and an all-round uniformity of performance was to be aimed at. Stage fussiness was to be banned. No movements or gesture were to be allowed except those dramatically significant. Our plays were to be Irish together with the best of continental drama.

Michael gathered about him a small group of potential actors and actresses, most of whom had no stage experience whatever. Mr and Mrs Sean Neeson were in charge of the Cork broadcasting station at the time and our rehearsals were held in the studio there. The station was in a wing of the disused Female Gaol in Sunday's Well where Michael had been imprisoned during the Civil War – drama for pleasure instead of pain. No producer that I ever came across threw himself into the job with such an intensity of nervous energy as our producer. At every rehearsal there was never the slightest doubt as to who was in control. 'Enthusiasm's the best thing. . . . Only we can't command it; fire and life are all, dead matter's nothing.' Michael's enthusiasm swept fire and life into a fair share of dead matter. Producing a play, composing a poem, attacking the subtleties of grammar – all called forth the same daemonic energy.

So *The Round Table*, with a curtain-raiser, *The Bear*, by Anton Chekhov, was staged at the Gregg Hall in Cork on 20 February 1928. It was a box-office success, and with the £20 or £30 which it earned for us we invested in a set of flats and the cast painted them a dove grey. Michael then set about realising an old ambition, to produce Chekhov's *Cherry Orchard*. That the only stage available to us was just about eighteen feet wide and ten feet deep, and that, except for a small door at the back, it was surrounded by a solid stone wall, did not deter him. The play was put into production and scheduled for a date in April, but in April Michael had to go to hospital to be operated upon for appendicitis and it was not staged until 7 May. In hospital, he told me, he had dispensed with the Confession which it was customary for patients to make prior to an operation.

No play, either before or after, was so popular with our players as *The Cherry Orchard*. Unfortunately their enthusiasm was not shared by the people of Cork. Audiences were small and our drama league ended up in debt. Still, we had a set of flats and Michael planned our third venture, *A Doll's House*, which he produced and acted in the following November. At first he had intended to play the part of Dr Rank, but an actor who was to have played Torvald Helmer went down with a bad attack of flu two days before the opening, and Michael took the part instead. It was quite a successful production, but it was to be the last in which he took an active part. Very soon after he went to Dublin as Librarian at Ballsbridge, and thereafter, apart from an occasional meeting in Cork or Dublin, he and I were only in contact by letter.

The Scholar-Gipsy

D. A. BINCHY

To be a poet is to have a soul in which knowledge passes instantaneously into feeling, and feeling flashes back as a new organ of knowledge.   GEORGE ELIOT

'You *must* meet him,' said AE to me – was it in 1927? 'You'll find him most exciting.' And some days later he arranged for both of us to have tea in his *Irish Statesman* office. It was a disastrous introduction. Over weak tea and stale biscuits we scowled at each other across the table, disagreeing violently on every subject, from the Irish Civil War to the merits of Heine's poetry. Our kindly host looked on half in dismay, half in amusement: even his unique capacity to spread sweetness and light was powerless against two very angry and very youthful know-alls.

How, from such unpromising beginnings, did we build a friendship which held steady through all the vicissitudes of life and waxed rather than waned as we both grew old? I think the original reason was that, even though we had had no difficulty in disliking each other at first sight, we shared a deep affection and veneration for two great men, who were themselves close friends: AE and Osborn Bergin, the first native scholar to achieve international pre-eminence in the field of Celtic Studies. Hence we were bound to meet from time to time in their company, and I remember it was Bergin who first called my attention to 'Guests of the Nation' ('Read that story,' he said; 'it's one that deserves to live.'). But more important was the fact that, after a number of false starts in different directions, I had just settled down to work at Celtic Studies under Bergin's direction. And that in itself was a sure passport to Michael's goodwill.

All his life he loved scholarship in Irish, and in later years it became almost an obsession with him, according to some of his admirers in Britain and America, who, understandably, deplored the increasing amount of time he devoted to it. It seemed as though his intense love of Ireland, combined with his antipathy to all the works and pomps of contemporary Irish society, drew him more and more to the study of the Irish past. Every relic of that past was dear to him. For years he waged war almost single-handed on the disgraceful indifference of a native government to the national monuments supposedly in its care, and also denounced the officially sponsored vandalism which is rapidly destroying the character of our cities. But more than all else he cherished the *Eigenart* of the Irish mind, the 'otherness' that expressed itself for so long in Irish and more recently in English. *Nil hibernici alienum —*

His unconcealed dislike of the modern Irish 'establishment' – political, ecclesiastical and linguistic – often led the pillars of our society to denounce him as a renegade. Nothing could be farther from the truth. On the contrary, he remained singularly faithful, in his fashion, to the ideals of his childhood. Nobody ever had less use for what von Hügel used to call the 'Officiality' of the Church; yet some of his most moving stories deal tenderly with the happier side of Irish Catholicism, and he was never without a succession of priest friends, from Paddy McSweeney and 'Tim' Traynor, the comrades of his early manhood, to Maurice Sheehy, whom he loved like a son during his last years. Similarly with his political nationalism. He might rage against Mr de Valera's Ireland, but woe betide anyone who dared to scoff at the idealism of those Republican soldiers by whose side he fought during the Civil War! *Experto crede*: this was a constant point of good-humoured friction between us.

It was the same with his attitude towards the Irish language. He had learned to speak it fluently in youth, and he never lost his love for it. But, like so many other early enthusiasts, he was revolted by the compulsion and commercialism which, after 1922, blighted the neo-Gaelic movement. And the essentially artificial nature of 'revivalist' writing led him to cherish all the more closely the Irish that was written throughout the centuries when it was really the native language – not, as nowadays, the 'national' language – of the writers. For this genuine Irish literature Michael retained all his original enthusiasm. He never tired of preaching to me and others like me that it was the duty of our generation, the last generation to have had the chance of learning the language from monoglot native speakers, to collect all the traditional material – poems, sagas, laws, homilies and the rest – and transmit it to posterity, properly edited and translated, *ad perpetuam rei memoriam*. Not that he made any extravagant claims for the Irish contribution to letters. A creative artist in his own mother-tongue, who was also widely read in the literature of other countries, he was far too expert and far too honest to over-value it. 'When he [Bryan Merryman] died in 1805 in a house on Clare Street, Limerick, Irish literature in the Irish language may be said to have died with him. From its beginnings among the monks of Clonmacnois and Glendalough to its end in Clare Street it was a literature of which no Irishman needs feel ashamed.' So ends his preface to *Kings, Lords, & Commons*.

Bergin used to lament that Michael had not been 'caught young' and put through the mill of scholastic discipline. But surely his temperament would have revolted against what Germans call *die Zunftwissenschaft*; indeed this might only have blunted the edge of his genius. For his approach to scholarship was primarily intuitive, and his intuition was at times so overwhelming as to leave a professional scholar gasping with amazement.

It was this that made collaboration with him an unforgettable experience. It was not merely his power to make you share his own excitement and enthusiasm. There was the fascination of

watching him wrestle with a problem which had baffled the professionals, and after a number of wildly false starts, produce the
right solution. 'Nonsense!' he would cry out against the received
translation. 'No poet would ever have said a thing like that. It
must be —' and he would propose something quite off the beam.
'Impossible, Michael, the grammar would be all wrong.' 'Well,
what about this?' And so on until, suddenly, the lightning struck
and you said to yourself half-incredulously: 'He's done it again.'

Needless to say this extraordinary gift was not confined to the
interpretation of obscure Irish texts. In his autobiography my
friend Sean O Faolain gives a very similar description of Michael
during their discussions on literature:

> His intuitive processes were something to marvel at, to distrust,
> and if one was wise, to respect profoundly, because if you were
> patient enough to discard the old boots and bits of seaweed that he
> would bring up from his deep diving, he was certain, sooner or
> later, to surface with a piece of pure gold.

It would be a profound error, however, to picture him as rely-
ing solely on his artistic inspiration. For over the years he had
acquired a solid capital of knowledge to feed that inspiration.
He worked tirelessly at Old and Middle Irish, so much so in fact
that professional scholars like myself were shamed by his wholly
disinterested pursuit of the subject we were paid to study. His
own copies of the texts were black with notes and cross-references;
how on earth did he manage to cram so much research into the
intervals between his own writing? After his death Harriet showed
me some massive notebooks into which he had copied the text of
sagas and poems from the editions of them that had appeared in
obscure and inaccessible journals. The text, be it noted, never the
accompanying translation: he could and would provide his own
translation.

And who could match him as a translator? No one has rendered
Irish poetry of all periods – Old, Middle and Modern – with such
perfect artistry. Small wonder that the reviewer of *Kings, Lords, &*

Commons in *The Times Literary Supplement* should have reckoned him among the great translators of our age. In that slim volume alone there are poems which will be read as long as Irish is studied – and, for all I know, long after Irish has disappeared.

Read, for example, the opening lines of 'Kilcash', which reproduce with almost uncanny effect not merely the mood of bewildered despair but even the verbal and metrical pattern of the original:

> *What shall we do for timber?*
> *The last of the woods is down.*
> *Kilcash and the house of its glory*
> *And the bell of the house are gone,*
> *The spot where that lady waited*
> *Who shamed all women for grace*
> *When earls came sailing to greet her*
> *And Mass was said in the place.*

Or travelling back five hundred years from this, listen to the Old Woman of Beare bemoaning the contrast between her passionate youth and the miseries of old age:

> *For my hands as you may see*
> *Are but bony wasted things,*
> *Hands that once would grasp the hand*
> *Clasp the royal neck of kings.*
>
> *I who had my day with kings*
> *And drank deep of mead and wine*
> *Drink wheywater with old hags*
> *Sitting in their rags and pine.*

A final example: only those who can savour the original of 'The Midnight Court' can fully appreciate the accuracy with which Frank O'Connor's translation catches the mood and the tempo of Merryman's rollicking lines:

> *You slut of ill-fame, allow your betters*
> *To tell the court how you learned your letters!*

Your seed and breed for all your brag
Were tramps to a man with rag and bag;
I knew your da and what passed for his wife,
And he shouldered his traps to the end of his life,
An aimless lout without friend or neighbour,
Knowledge or niceness, wit or favour:
The breeches he wore were riddled with holes
And his boots without a tack of the soles.
Believe me, friends, if you sold at a fair,
Himself and his wife, his kids and gear,
When the costs were met, by the Holy Martyr,
You'd still go short for a glass of porter.

Incidentally, this superb rendering of 'The Midnight Court' was banned for years by the Irish Censors as 'indecent or obscene', while the Irish original it so faithfully reproduces was permitted to circulate freely. Michael used to laugh over this typical anomaly of the modern Irish scene: obviously the Censors were satisfied that for ninety-five per cent of the population the poem composed in the 'national language' would remain in safe and decent obscurity.

I have written here only of his work on the literature of Gaelic Ireland. Others far better qualified will have paid their tribute to the master of the short story, the sensitive and generous critic, the enthralling conversationalist. But his scholar friends, too, who have received from him far more than they could give him, claim space to acknowledge their indebtedness. This indebtedness will be increased, I hope, before long, when two important books which he had completed before his death are published.

I myself am conscious of an even deeper debt. It was Michael's glowing interest in every branch of Irish scholarship that encouraged me to persevere with my own work. For despite the old poet's praise of a scholar's life – *aoibheann beatha an scolaire!* – I have often found myself querying both its purpose and its value. Once, in a moment of depression, I recalled to him that bitter verse of Yeats which seemed to me to define with merciless clarity the great gulf that is fixed between the scholar and the artist.

> *Bald heads forgetful of their sins,*
> *Old, learned, respectable bald heads*
> *Edit and annotate the lines*
> *That young men, tossing on their beds,*
> *Rhymed out in love's despair*
> *To flatter beauty's ignorant ear.*

Michael's reaction was, as usual, vigorous. 'Rubbish!' he said. 'That's a totally unreal contrast. Your old Irish jurists were far wiser than W.B. when they numbered among the *áes dána* (artists) not merely the poet but the scholar and the craftsman, for each of them needs the same divine spark if he's to be really good at his job.'

Did he speak from conviction or out of pure kindness, seeking to comfort a despondent friend? In any event those words have ever since aided and encouraged me to continue. This was easy while he was still with us. But now that he has gone and I can no longer be cheered by his unflagging sympathy, the old doubts begin to recur. It is a measure of the hold this extraordinary man had, and continues to have, on all his friends that whenever I feel tempted to bid farewell to the old Irish jurists and spend my few remaining years in an effort to recapture the joys of classical literature, I seem to hear that unforgettable voice quoting from a poem we both loved:

> *Why falterest thou? I wandered till I died.*
> *Roam on! The light we sought is shining still.*

Michael-Frank

RICHARD ELLMANN

In the late spring of 1946, having crossed the Atlantic only to find myself even more at sea in Ireland, I had the luck to meet Frank O'Connor, who gave me my bearings. He encouraged me to visit and I was touched by this indulgent attitude towards my unseemly profession, which was that of graduate student. I came to understand that his private life was not conducted on hierarchical principles, and that he put no stock in public estimates. He had been a rebel, and doubly so, for within the movement he remained a nonconformist. He opposed oratory and posturing. Though his beautiful speech cried out that he was Irish, and from Cork, he was impatient of that verbal parade to which nationality, religion or politics muster us.

Michael had, in fact, a fine impudence towards all obsessive thinking. The theme of 'Guests of the Nation' was one he hit on naturally, for no one knew better than he how patriotism could gather itself into a dogma that overrode decency. In many of his stories the enemy is not evil but incrustation, not only on the national but on the familial level. So he could display in 'The Luceys' the foolish victory of dogged paternal pride over thoughtless affection. And yet, obstinate himself, Michael understood being deadset on something, and could respect the old woman in 'The Long Road to Ummera' who would not be buried anywhere in the world but the one place. I think he caught, in 'The Star that Bids the Shepherd Fold', the points of view expressed by the old Irish priest and the French sea captain, the one spiritually and the other physically intolerant; while Michael preferred the second, he saw it as almost equally narrow. That people moved or, rather, faltered among fixed ideas was something O'Connor recognized, yet he longed for gestures that should be less impeded. He did what he could to prevent cruelty or tightmindedness from masquerading as high principle. He wanted life to be something other than martyrdom to either a public or a private religion. It should be free and impulsive, as purely unintimidated as the teacher in 'The Bridal Night', who risks contumely to lie in the bed beside her delirious lover.

Michael had spent a year in Cork Gaol and a prison camp, and so he knew as well as hated the curtailment of liberty. When I saw him last, in the spring of 1964, he was explaining to an audience at Trinity College that Ireland, in his view, had made little progress on this front, the only one that really mattered. Yet in his own life he had repeatedly worked free from restraints imposed by a broken home and a wretched education. He studied languages, becoming proficient in at least three, he achieved some expertness in architecture and history as well as literature. He had only to see a shut door to feel impelled to open it. At the time of our first meeting he was writing a book on Shakespeare, the first of his three books of criticism. He propounded some of his theories to John Kelleher of Harvard and me, and I am abashed to remember that he gave us some alarm. One night he would sweep away, as interpolations, the witch scenes in *Macbeth*, and another he would body forth an unknown but, he assured us, perfectly conjurable collaborator of Shakespeare in the problem comedies. Our trepidation had fortunately no effect on him, and his learned boldness is one of the many merits of *The Road to Stratford*. He there asserts that *Edward III* 'is a play supposed by Tucker Brooke to be by Peele, by Robertson to be Greene's; by some Shakespearean scholars to contain two acts of Shakespeare. I have no doubt whatever that the play is entirely Shakespeare's.' To be at variance with Tucker Brooke was at that time scarcely conceivable for me, who had studied with that formidable authority.

But today Michael's position, if not susceptible of verification (any more than Brooke's), is more tenable, and the disputation is part of the book's freshness and insouciant scholarship.

Though some people thought Michael flamboyant in his views, he did not so regard himself. He thought he was stating conclusions that nobody in his right mind could miss. The strength of *The Mirror in the Roadway* and *The Lonely Voice* comes from this assumptive power. It begins in close observation, of course, but then, in an almost visionary way, renders writers, objects and themes malleable. Whoever the writer he discusses, O'Connor will not release him until he has yielded up the network of interconnecting passageways between behavior in society and talent at his desk. O'Connor's critical writing is hungry to judge, and unsatisfied unless it is deciphering a writer's mysteries, not necessarily mysteries of uneasy collaboration with another, as in Shakespeare's case, but mysteries of uneasy collaboration with an inner self. If he is bold, he is also subtle, as when he uncovers the 'moral hysteria' of Jane Austen in *Mansfield Park*, or says of the mayor's garden in *Le Rouge et le noir*, 'Any real-estate agent worth his salt could give us a clearer impression of the property of Monsieur de Renal than Stendhal.' He noted with regret that the novel in our time has gone behind Stendhal's mirror, by becoming self-absorbed, indifferent to that crowd which in the nineteenth century it had so brilliantly particularized. In Henry James's work he saw the switch occurring, and depicted it in one of those enviable figures that seemed to flow from him without effort:

> To students of the novel, James is interesting principally as the transition figure between the classical novel and the modern novel. Somewhere in his work the change takes place between the two; somewhere the ship has been boarded by pirates, and when at last it comes into harbor, nobody could recognize in its rakish lines the respectable passenger ship that set sail from the other side of the water. The passengers would seem to have been murdered on the way, and there is nothing familiar about the dark foreign faces that peer at us over the edge.

c

He understood what James was doing, admired it somewhat, but did not follow. He saw that his own art must radiate out from a single nucleus, must not attempt detachment or alien centers-of-consciousness in the manner of James or Joyce.

He felt himself, nonetheless, to be in reaction against one nineteenth-century aspect, romantic color and extravagance. Often he humorously pretended to discount his own views as those of 'a tough-skinned old realist' or of 'an old-fashioned realist'. Of one of his characters he says approvingly, 'The real world was trouble enough for him.' He encouraged Yeats to see him as more a realist than in fact he was, and for a time Yeats praised O'Connor for his sharp Corkman's eye, then, more knowledgeably, for his Chekhovian inspection of Irish life. The last romantic and the last realist found they had much in common. When they served together as directors of the Abbey Theatre, they surprised each other by a fairly steady agreement about plays or persons. Another bond became evident when O'Connor made his translations from Irish and Old Irish poetry. The gauntly expressed passions in them won Yeats over; he arranged for his sisters to publish them at the Cuala Press, and he graciously notified O'Connor that some of the good lines were making their way into his own poems. In exchange he proposed some revisions, to which O'Connor responded by dedicating the book to Yeats.

Yeats gradually accepted and even relished their imaginative affinity. Once he read a new poem, about the Hermit Ribh, to O'Connor and another writer, then asked if they understood it. The other man said he had, but O'Connor burst out, 'I didn't understand a bloody word.' The following day Yeats recounted the conversation: 'The man who said he understood everything had understood nothing, while O'Connor had understood everything.' The next of Yeats's 'Supernatural Songs' probably reflected the incident by beginning, 'What matter that you understand no word!' Such communication with Yeats, on a sub-verbal level, enabled Michael to write the essay about him in the *Yale Review* of some years back, which remains the best portrait we have, outdistancing the strenuous efforts of several generations of writers and scholars.

When I heard that Michael would be lecturing at Harvard in the summer of 1952, I persuaded him to warm up at Northwestern. He agreed, and spent the spring in Evanston, liking it so well that he was prevailed upon to return the following spring. In some ways he discountenanced the United States, which he saw now for the first time. One couldn't, for example, take a walk in this impossible country. The streets had no footpaths, there was no way of walking uninterruptedly along the lake front. It was clear that we failed of being Dublin, let alone of being Cork. Yet as always he struck up friendships: Sunday mornings he walked with Fred Faverty, a scholar of Matthew Arnold; in the afternoon he might be asked to sample an exotic dish (in spite of his vaunted preference for Irish cooking) which Daniel Weiss, in between constructing a mummy case and writing a dissertation on Lawrence's Oedipus complex, had concocted; or he might visit Walter Scott, whose parodies of Gide and others he admired. He was the comfort of our household, cheering us up as our first child bawled above our heads and our poodle howled beside us, commenting with the same humorous opinionativeness about pediatric as about literary problems.

Mrs Yeats used to call him Michael-Frank, combining his private and literary selves in one affectionate nickname. There was in fact no hyphen between the two, no impulsion to play artist or reluctance to be man. When he repeatedly revised his work, before publication and after, he did so not only to make it more wrought, but more free; for all that he had learned with desperate acquisitiveness stood in the way of primary apprehension. Over and over he started again, until the sense of struggle was supplanted by one of exhilaration. This he achieved also in his own person, a sense that came to friends as to readers not only from his arrowing mind but from the great bow of his being, now reposeful now taut.

Human Contact in the Short Stories

DEBORAH AVERILL

A reader of Frank O'Connor's stories notices at once their atmosphere of warm intimacy. His concern with human contact originates in his sense of human isolation and it pervades his work; characters continuously touch each other, lie in bed discussing their problems or fall in love, and the narrative itself reflects a lively compassion which gives these stories their distinctive relevance.

Remarks he made about other writers and passages from his own stories indicate that he sometimes found his imaginative powers nearly overwhelming. His aspiration to live 'above and beyond' himself brought the sense of emptiness and uncertainty which accompanies any creative act. His insight into Jane Austen's sensibility may have some application to his own: 'If I read her rightly she was a woman afraid of the violence of her own emotions . . .' He prefaces *The Lonely Voice*, his book of essays on the short story, with a sentence from Pascal which he often refers to: 'The eternal silence of those infinite spaces terrifies me.' This mood of loneliness, fear and desolation lies behind his efforts at contact and gives direction to his creative activity.

His perceptions of emptiness lead him to seek an intensification of life. He delights in sheer animal vitality and encourages a full, waking life of the senses. In his introduction to *The Fountain of Magic* he admires an early Irish poet because he 'was eager for sensation rather than for thought; the D. H. Lawrence of his own day, he had no head for philosophy but created a natural world of pure sensation, which is magical because all sensation is magic, and what is most intensely felt in literature is what we have not been able to explain – most often a memory of childhood, of house or field or face'. He dislikes abstractions, 'the Greek reasoning about life which are our daily bread', and thinks they have crippled modern literature as well as modern society by creating artificial barriers to communication. He tries to create an attitude of mind informed from within, from nature and the 'inner light', to overcome the literal application of sterile social mores, theories or religious doctrines. Consequently he avoids abstract speculation or burdening character or incident with a larger intellectual framework than is provided by the situation itself in relation to general human experience. He shows annoyance at Edmund Wilson's essay on Turgenev's story 'The Watch', because Wilson interprets the watch as a symbol of 'the antiquated social system' or 'the corruption of old Russia'. O'Connor says: 'I shouldn't like to think that something which seems to move only from within is really being moved from outside by the desire to teach a lesson.'

He tries to locate within the complex, reflecting man the warm, vital animal which needs and seeks contact with others. His imagination dwells on the blood-ties which bind the human community together, on heredity, sex, reproduction, the family as an organic unit – the natural processes and conditions which create and sustain life. These natural relationships underlie and enhance human contact, so that it becomes not merely an interchange of ideas, but a communion, a sharing of experience expressed in the concrete acts of speaking and touching. What he says about D. H. Lawrence applies to his own work as well:

> What must be said about these … stories is that the physical contact in them is precisely what gives them their warmth and joy, and one might argue that the physical contact bears a strong resemblance to what we know as Christian charity. By the act of touching we accept our neighbor's dirt and smells and sores and

brutality as Christ accepted them and in order that our own may be forgiven us.

He summarizes his ideas about the short story as a genre in his introduction to *The Lonely Voice*. Because it deals with submerged population groups, with people who cannot or will not exist in a normal relationship to society, it reflects an intense awareness of human loneliness. It is 'romantic, individualistic, and intransigent', outside time, embracing past, present and future in a few well-chosen moments 'lit by an unearthly glow'. Yet O'Connor's stories in particular convey a strong sense of family and community ties. They are remote from society, but not divorced from it; we can always feel a need for companionship, a pull towards contact and reintegration, and a desire to work out ways or reconciliation within the span of the individual life. He celebrates marriage as the institution in which natural bonds can best be maintained; at its best it combines romantic love with social acceptability. His attitude towards the more anti-social aspects of sexual contact is ambivalent; though he asserts a need for naturalness, liberation of the senses and experimentation, he recognizes at the same time the dangers of promiscuity. Not only does it bring unwanted children into the world, but it perverts and wastes creative energy, making contact meaningless and automatic.

His concern with human contact can be seen in his method of characterization. In *The Lonely Voice* he says that short-story characters are Little Men, people who lack generality; while we identify with at least one character in a novel, we don't identify with anyone in a short story; we can't really see into their minds and so they remain separate from us. Their identities are largely determined by their circumstances, by the necessities of their lives; they act either from habit, social pressure or their own natural impulses and desires. His view of human nature is thus deterministic, minimizing inner conflict, self-knowledge and individual choice. His characters are innocents because they are overwhelmed by the vast implications of choosing good or evil. When they do transcend their circumstances, they do so in terms of contact, in their relations with other people. He writes of loneliness, but not aloneness. A solitary character for O'Connor has no real identity; he is cut loose from life, from everything that gives meaning to his existence.

O'Connor frequently casts his mind back to a childhood world for inspiration, because that period of his life exercised the most compulsive hold on him and because children have not yet lost their naturalness and innocence. His autobiography, *An Only Child*, ends when he reaches manhood. He often personifies himself as a child and rarely writes in the first person unless he is recreating aspects of his childhood or youth. This use of the child character gives him a manageable way of treating important and threatening conflicts.

In 'The Study of History', for example, the antithesis between imagination and reality is presented in terms of identity and resolved in terms of contact. When Larry, the child-genius, learns where babies come from, he realizes that his parents' marriage was not an event ordained from creation but 'one of those apparently trivial events that are no more than accidents, but have the effect of changing the destiny of humanity'. He speculates about his ancestors on both sides of the family and wonders what would have happened if the circumstances of his life had been different. When he visits one of his father's old girl friends to see what she would have been like as a mother, her physical presence impresses him as no imaginary person could have done. He feels guilty and wretched because of the jealousy his visit evokes in his own mother. That night, when he is in bed and alone with the infinite possibilities he has unearthed, he becomes terrified. He tries to soothe himself as he usually does when he has let his imagination run wild, by going over the facts he knows about himself: 'I am Larry Delaney, and my mother is Mary Delaney, and we live in Number 8 Wellington Square . . .' But this time it doesn't work: 'It was as if my own identity was a sort of sack I had to live in, and I had deliberately worked my way out of it, and now I couldn't get back again because I had grown too big for it . . . I was away in the middle of empty space, divorced from my mother and home and everything permanent and familiar.' He cries until his mother comes in. By touching her, holding her hand, he reassures himself: 'I could not tell her of the nightmare in which I was lost. Instead, I took her hand, and gradually the terror retreated, and I became myself again, shrank into my little skin of identity, and left infinity and all its anguish behind.'

Since domestic family life, with its intimacy, its frank, familiar give-and-take and its spontaneous hitting or caressing, provides a secure refuge from loneliness, O'Connor feels keenly the tragedy of the illegitimate child. 'The Babes in the Wood' is a sombre story about Terry, a pathetic child who doesn't realize what is lacking in his life until he finds out what real contact can mean; he falls asleep in the arms of the man who has said he will marry Terry's mother and take them both to England. The moment of contact heightens the sense of desolation when the child is finally left for good with the old woman who takes care of him.

O'Connor's adult characters, like his children, are lonely innocents who determine their identity through contact. They reach from the changing complexities of their lives towards some kind of rooted primary condition in which they find rest and unity at least temporarily. Contact with others draws them out of themselves; the imperfect struggling animal in them impels them to overcome barriers to communication. To make his characters approachable, O'Connor often deflates them by using mock-heroic techniques; he tends towards caricature, towards a gentle puncturing of dignified poses and a revelation of the absurd.

He often contrasts characters who communicate easily with those who don't. The former are frank, self-revealing and naturally intimate, the latter are cautious and reticent. The two personality types can be seen in 'The Sorcerer's Apprentice' and 'The Cheapjack'. In 'The Sorcerer's Apprentice' Una discovers, through sexual contact, a new vitality and inner harmony which allow her to repudiate the inhibitions imposed by small-town life and her Catholic conscience, and to achieve a new identity as Denis's wife. Denis can produce this change in her because she is open to new influences and because he is a fatherly man who feels at ease with women and invites their confidences. Because Denis's divorce is not recognized in Ireland, they must become exiles in England, but the success of the individual relationship transcends the rejection by the community.

In 'The Cheapjack', Sam Higgins, the schoolteacher, fails to win Nancy McCann, a widow and fellow-teacher, because of his reticent manner. He is dry, cautious, ironic and always conscious of his dignity; even Carmody, his rival for Nancy, can't stimulate him to break out of himself and court her. Instead he shows his emotion in indirect, childish ways. His isolation nearly drives him mad. When he finally does break free and make contact, he does so in a negative way which perverts and destroys his love; he reads to his class Carmody's diary containing intimate details of the love affair he should have been living through himself. They fight, and Sam, having disgraced himself, is forced to leave town. Unlike Una, he has failed to make contact with anyone, and he simply vanishes. He has no identity left at all and forfeits even the company of his sister Delia.

In stories like the two just discussed, the situation arises from a localized set of circumstances, a particular provincial environment, and from the interaction of specific types of personalities. As a result the emotion is too slack and the characters' plights fail to engage the reader as thoroughly as they should. In his best stories O'Connor gives his imagination freer rein and interprets the situation in terms of general human conditions and necessities. Personality becomes less important; impulses and desires are transformed into single passions or forces which dominate character and make it memorable. Human contact, seen as a prelude to prolonged or permanent separation, takes on a poignancy which illuminates the entire lives of the characters involved.

'The Bridal Night' concerns a young man, Denis, whose hopeless love for the local schoolteacher makes him show increasingly violent signs of insanity. The night before he is to be removed permanently to an asylum, he calls for her and falls asleep peacefully and innocently in her arms. The moment of contact and the single-mindedness of his love carry him outside time; his mother says, 'I declare for the time being I felt 'twas worth it all, all the troubles of his birth and rearing and all the lonesome years ahead.' In 'Guests of the Nation' the young soldier who has formed a close friendship with two English hostages is forced by the rules of war to help kill them. The intense horror of the act, its violation of every natural impulse, immediately deepens the idea of contact and transforms the friendship into a paradigm of human brotherhood, the boy into an instrument of death. Something dies in him as well; like Larry in 'The Study of History' he is 'away in the middle of empty space': '. . . I was somehow very small and very lost and lonely like a child astray in the snow. And anything that happened to me afterwards, I never felt the same about again.'

In 'The Long Road to Ummera' the old woman is sure that after death she will reassume an earlier, happier identity and meet her husband and neighbours. She thinks her body must be returned to the village where she was born; the physical proximity of the graves will insure her reintegration into her former community. The sheer force of her passion contrasts with her lifelessness; her body is ugly and withered, her senses are unresponsive, and her heartbeat has slowed to a faint rhythm. Her faith projects itself beyond life and she contacts her dead husband; she sees him once before her journey, beckoning to her, and again as she lies on her death-bed, when she shouts to him: 'Be easy now, my brightness, my own kind loving comrade. I'm coming. After all the long years I'm on the road to you at last . . .'

O'Connor's concern with human contact influences not only his characterizations but his narrative technique as well. He says in *The Lonely Voice*: 'I once tried to describe my own struggle with the form by saying that "Generations of skilful stylists from Chekhov to Katherine Mansfield and James Joyce had so fashioned the short story that it no longer rang with the tone of a man's voice speaking".' His attempt to recreate the effect of a speaking voice, which he considers the physical body of a story, reflects a desire for direct contact and communication with the reader. He criticizes Hemingway's style because 'by repetition of key words and phrases it slows down the whole conversational movement of prose, the casual, sinuous, evocative quality that distinguishes it from poetry and is intended to link author and reader in a common perception of the object'. He designs the voice to convey a sense of both human nearness and human separateness.

The narrators through whom he tells his stories are loosely defined personae who are always either implicitly or explicitly present. They are not bound to a consistent point of view, so that they can speak either as a near-by witness of the situation, like a fellow-villager, or as an omnipresent creator, a kind of angelic observer. They move freely in and out of the characters' minds without identifying completely with anyone; even in stories told from only one person's point of view, we can see him from the outside as well as the inside.

In 'The Cheapjack', for example, the narrator is a fellow-villager who likes and admires Sam Higgins. He speaks in his own person at the beginning and end, but tells most of the story from Sam's point of view, only leaving him for a moment to observe Delia and Nancy talking in the kitchen. His final ironic description of Sam as 'honest' reveals how imperfectly he knows him, and enhances the pathos of Sam's loneliness: 'We were all sorry for him. Poor Sam! As decent a man as ever drew breath, but too honest, too honest!'

Again, in 'The Babes in the Wood', we look through Terry's eyes for most of the story; his inarticulate feeling of desertion is far more telling than an objective description would be. At the end, however, the point of view shifts to Florrie and then to the narrator, who draws away from his characters. His brief revelation of himself as a solitary, compassionate observer of the scene extends the mood of helpless desolation: 'She put her arms around him and he fell asleep, but she remained solemnly holding him, looking at him with detached and curious eyes. He was hers at last. There were no more rivals. She fell asleep too and did not notice the evening train go up the valley. It was all lit up. The evenings were drawing in.'

The tone of the stories is conversational, animated and evocative, embodying O'Connor's own energetic vitality. It is intended to elicit an immediate emotional response from the reader. The language and idiom come directly from the situation. There is little obscure symbolism, stylization or abstract speculation. His easy, confident fluency creates a deceptive impression of casual off-handedness; he often narrates tragic events as if they were everyday occurrences which didn't really matter, but the underlying involvement builds up force until it is released at the moment of crisis in a passage which is overtly emotional, intimate and intense. Sometimes when these passages are too subjective and unrestrained they fail to be as convincing as he intended; he is too prone to making sweeping statements like 'I was a stranger to her, and nothing I could ever do would make us the same to one another again.'

He makes his greatest impact when he counterpoints the warm familiarity of the speaking voice with strict objective controls. Sometimes he uses a dramatic scene instead of the narrative to express insight. He thinks a 'sharp contrast should ideally exist between narrative and drama – the former should be subjective and persuasive, the latter objective and compulsive – in the one the storyteller suggests to the reader what he believes happened, in the other he proves to him that this is in fact how it did happen'. In 'The Mad Lomasneys', when Rita realizes she has married the wrong man, the utter hopelessness of her position is made clear during a conversation with her sister and Ned, the man she should have married.

O'Connor achieves chilling effects of distance by treating time and place in a way which suggests 'the eternal silence of those infinite spaces'. Sometimes he endues ordinary, familiar settings with a quality of remoteness which makes the living individual seem to shrink and flounder; efforts at contact become highly charged. The description of the bogland in 'Guests of the Nation' is of this kind: 'It was all mad lonely with nothing but a patch of lantern light between ourselves and the dark, and birds screeching and hollering all around, disturbed by the guns.' In 'In the Train' all Ireland contracts until it becomes a tiny image of itself: 'And while they talked the train dragged across a dark plain, the heart of Ireland, and in the moonless night tiny cottage-windows blew past like sparks from a fire, and a pale simulacrum of the lighted carriages leaped and frolicked over hedges and fields.'

Sometimes he distances events temporarily; the narrator speaks in an empty present of things that happened long before and which outweigh anything that has happened to the characters since. The future becomes subservient to the past, and the immediacy of the speaking voice is tempered by the backward pull of events. In 'The Bridal Night' the old woman talks to the narrator about something that took place twelve years earlier. Since that time she has been alone, and has visited her son in the asylum only once. The contact in the present between the narrator and the woman takes its significance from the earlier contact between Denis and the schoolteacher.

Although O'Connor sometimes fails to make human contact more than a momentary reprieve from inner conflict and intellectual complexities, at his best he fashions his stories into effective, lasting vehicles for communicating experience and uniting author and reader in a recognition of their shared humanity. He refines the idea of contact as the most significant response the living can make to the empty uncertainty of separation and death.

Frank O'Connor in Harvard

RICHARD T. GILL

I

When Frank O'Connor was teaching at the Harvard Summer School in the early 1950s, he sometimes spoke of establishing a permanent school of writing in the United States. It typified his feeling about Americans. He thought they were wonderfully talented, imaginative people, well worth any effort put into them. He also thought they were badly in need of instruction about literature and life. The dual attitude persisted through the ten years he spent intermittently in this country. He was delighted by the brilliance of American life and skeptical of its glitter. He wrote of 'the superiority of the American short story over all others that I know', but he also thought that most American writers did not know the first thing about what a short story was or how it should be constructed.

However much the idea of a school for American writers may have appealed to him, it was not a project that he himself could ever have undertaken. Teaching took too much out of him, both physically and spiritually. He explained it by saying that he became so involved in his students' work that he completely lost sight of his own. During his visits to the United States he taught at Northwestern, Harvard and Stanford universities, either in the summer sessions or in isolated semesters during the academic year. His schedule usually involved a course in the techniques of short-story writing and a course of lectures on some topic such as the nineteenth-century novel or aspects of Irish literature. It was in the writing course that his identification with his students was so strong. 'It's a beautiful story,' he'd say about an idea of one of his students. 'In fact, that girl is simply bursting with beautiful stories. The trouble is, she isn't writing them. She's running away from them every time. Now if I were writing that story what I'd do would be to start the whole thing back ten years.' And then he'd sketch out his version of the story which, in fact, he'd have written mentally from beginning to end.

The lecture courses wore him down in a different way. There was, first of all, the problem of preparation. Like all good writers, O'Connor always dropped whatever he was doing when an idea for a new short story struck. The result was that when he arrived at the university to begin teaching, his lecture notes were usually far from complete. Since he also had the writing course to do, and since he had many American friends with whom he spent hours talking and singing folk songs and Mozart arias, there was often a late-night rush to get his materials in order. Also, as he discovered, there were some special hazards in American life. One Sunday during his second summer at Harvard, his friend, the late critic Horace Reynolds, took him for a stroll around Walden Pond, the haunt of the great Thoreau. It was a lovely day, but neither Reynolds nor O'Connor had counted on the American mosquito, who saw the undefended visitor from abroad and all but carried him bodily across the Pond. It was a sad sight indeed to see O'Connor trying to lecture on the nineteenth-century novel that next morning, his jaw unshaven and swollen like a balloon, his eyes glazed from the medicines that had been pumped into him to keep him among the living. Even the glories of *Pride and Prejudice* couldn't stir his interest that day!

But it was also a question of his exalted view of what a proper lecture course should be. When it came to writing, O'Connor was always quite authoritative – deeply serious about the job, but never really awed by it. University lectures, however, were something else again, and this, I believe, was the one and only respect in which his own lack of a formal education showed through. In any sense in which the word has significance at all, O'Connor was a deeply educated man. But he was not formally educated and he sometimes assumed an eminence in the works of a university that is not always found in reality. What this meant was that he could never toss off a course of lectures in the way the professionals do and in fact sometimes have to do if they are to survive.

If preparing his lectures took a great deal out of him, however, the results were often quite striking. Of course, O'Connor had an enormous asset simply in his physical presence. When he came to the United States to teach in 1952, he was at the height of his powers in every way. He was forty-nine; he was writing brilliantly and had just put together *The Stories of Frank O'Connor*; he was in good health. Standing before a lecture audience with his silver-grey hair, his dark eyebrows, his eyes peering through black-rimmed glasses that always looked too small for the strong, masculine face, he was an arresting figure. When he spoke, the response was immediate, for his voice was most impressive. It was not just the depth of it – though it was a very deep voice and he could sing a low D with ease – but the cadence and rhythm of his speech and also his cultivated and yet unaffected accent and choice of words. He himself was well aware of the possibilities of oral expression and he often told about the time he first heard a playback of a story he had read on the radio and how much he had learned from the experience.

The most striking thing about the content of his lectures was the absolutely fresh, newly-arrived-at view they gave of the subject at hand. The weakness of this approach was that it demanded so much of him. Since he had little recourse to the general critical literature of the field and drew constantly on his own resources, the lectures, particularly towards the end of the semester, were sometimes thin. Also, they were works-in-progress rather than finished products. The writings O'Connor later based on his lectures are generally more polished and well-organized than were the lectures themselves. That splendid book on the modern novel,

The Mirror in the Roadway, represents not simply a repetition but a substantial development and generalization of what he had taught in class. In another sense, however, the in-progress quality of the lectures was their great strength. For what the students were witnessing was the effort of a man of extraordinary insight, honesty and wisdom to understand matters of passionate concern to himself. It was a dull student who, hearing those lectures, did not begin to share that passion and to gain some small understanding of the intense commitment Frank O'Connor had made in his life – a commitment of which all of us are the beneficiaries.

II

His writing courses were handled quite differently and he was probably always slightly more at home with them. These courses are of considerable interest because they brought out the well-considered views on short-story construction of one of the greatest modern practitioners of the art. O'Connor never really wrote this down. The closest he came was in his book on the short story, *The Lonely Voice*. But the emphasis in the book has shifted from the practical to the analytic, while the course itself was wholly practical. It was also, it might be said, a quite new and sometimes shattering experience for the students taking it.

The class was usually small, twenty students or under, of all ages and professions, each selected on the basis of previously submitted work. There were no lectures, but only class discussion, and this class discussion was focused on the students' work in a rather specific way. Each student was required to submit his idea for a short story to the class for its 'approval' before he could begin writing it. This raised the interesting possibility that a student might not get the class's approval and hence would be taking a writing course in which he was officially not allowed to do any writing. Furthermore, after a draft of a story had been written, it would be read aloud by O'Connor to the class as a whole and subjected to his and their public criticisms.

D

For many members of his classes this approach to short-story writing was shocking and, for some, it remained so to the end. All the people who took the courses were aspiring writers. All had committed some part of their self-esteem to the view that if they were not good writers at least they were not all that bad either. Many, especially some of the older students, had been working for years in private, and the very taking of the course was an act of desperation undoubtedly regretted many times before the classes actually met. In these circumstances the notion of having to submit one's efforts to public scrutiny could not have been more alarming.

Why did O'Connor arrange things this way? Why, especially since he often contrasted the public art of the theater with the lonely, private art of the short story, did he not give more shelter to his apprentices? Of course, he did give shelter. Whenever he felt that the class was moving in an obviously wrong direction, he stepped in. If his course was a democracy at all, it was most definitely a *guided* democracy. Still, the class reaction was important because it provided a necessary symbol of objectivity. What O'Connor knew – and what his students soon learned – was how easy it is in private to confuse the personal but nevertheless universal with the merely personal. Many of the students were astonished to see how ideas that they had thought absolutely stunning could fall so flat in view of their class-mates. It was a gross test – the class could be wrong and so could O'Connor – but it did give a sense of reality to efforts that might otherwise have remained internal and obscure.

The most difficult problem, of course, was establishing the criteria by which stories were to be judged, and it is here that O'Connor's strong and really quite explicit sense of what a short story was came through. The central concept was that of the 'theme': a statement of the complete story boiled down to 'no more than four lines'. Occasionally he relented and allowed six lines, but anything more than six was bad news and certain to bring forth his displeasure.

The search for proper 'themes' usually occupied the first third or half of an O'Connor writing course and it proved endlessly fascinating and baffling. A superb theme in the class's view would bring nothing but a shrug from the master. A few minutes later he would turn back to one of the themes no one had paid the least attention to. 'Who was it who wrote this?' he'd ask with a rather curious expression. 'In my opinion, it's an absolute masterpiece.' And the class would be gasping at the marvel of it.

The element in a theme that O'Connor stressed most frequently was that of incident. At times he virtually defined a theme as an incident in which the people involved become basically changed. In the last sentence of his famous early story, 'Guests of the Nation', he has the narrator say: 'And anything that happened to me afterwards, I never felt the same about again.' Or, as he put it later, there is a 'bending of the iron bar'. When, as a result of the central incident, everything in a man's life is changed, then, in O'Connor's view, the writer has a real story in his grasp.

This isn't quite the whole of the matter, but it was the approach O'Connor started his classes with, and we can see already that he was ruling out a number of apparently reasonable alternatives. One thing he was ruling out, for example, was any story based centrally on the traits or idiosyncrasies of the main character. Themes that began 'There was this beautiful, warm-hearted, but also proud and rather secretive young woman ...' were quite unacceptable. One of the main reasons for the 'no more than four lines' edict was precisely that words like 'warm-hearted', 'proud', 'secretive', and so on, would have to be left out for lack of space. The underlying purpose, of course, was to guarantee that the central incident would be as universal as possible. If the story is conceivable only on the assumption that the heroine is 'warm-hearted', it is less universal than if it works independently of the state of her heart. If, in addition, she must also necessarily be 'proud' and 'secretive', then the writer is no longer telling about an incident of general significance: he is describing a particular character.

O'Connor had no general objection to writing about particular characters, but he did not believe it could be done in the short-story *form*. If the writer was basically beginning with a character instead of an incident, he was, in O'Connor's view, setting out to write not a short story but a novel. This was one of several important distinctions O'Connor made between these two forms. It can be justified on the grounds that, in the novel, the writer has the time and space to explore the full ramifications of a person's character, whereas in the short story he has not. This, however, is not the main thing since, as he stressed, there are some short stories that are longer than novels. It is closer to his view to put the matter the other way around – to say that the relative lengths of the two forms are dictated by the different objectives that each sets out to achieve. And it was characteristic of O'Connor to believe that writing, like music, did come in particular forms, and that to confuse these forms was to court serious trouble.

By emphasizing the relative universality of the short-story form, however, O'Connor faced another problem with his students. Themes would come in that weren't stories at all but abstract generalizations. A student once submitted as a theme (either in humor or in desperation) the quotation, 'The quality of mercy is not strained.' Another wanted to write on 'Pride goeth before a fall'. More common, and more complicated, was the symbolic theme, the characteristic feature of which was that the behavior of the characters is limited not by what their human responses are likely to be in the given situation but by what a pre-viously determined pattern of symbolism has dictated. O'Connor ruled these out too, usually citing Joyce (a writer who fascinated, irritated and disturbed him all his life) as an example of how *not* to go about writing short stories.

The rejection of symbolic stories brought a great outcry from many of his students each year, and they could, of course, point to dozens of examples of modern stories that took the symbolic rather than the realistic route. O'Connor was unperturbed. He was ultimately teaching his classes the lessons that had been important to him in his own experience and in that experience symbolism had proved a dead-end. His own stories were based on actual events that had happened to him or that he had heard about happening to others. Only rarely would he even go so far as to imagine a possible event, and that is still quite a different thing from conscious symbolism which he saw as nothing but an intellectual limitation on the richness of the world of experience. His ultimate aim was a fusion of the subjective and the objective. He feared too much objectivity, which led to 'naturalism'. But he saw even greater dangers in the internalized world of the symbolist who tried to make reality conform to an intellectual pattern.

So the symbolists were hushed (for the moment at least) and the search for themes went on. At times it seemed to his students that the search was hopeless, since every possible statement could be ruled out on some ground or other. There was the 'political' theme, charged with social significance, but tending to the intellectual and the abstract. There was the 'so what' theme that had event, but no change. There was the 'too bad' theme that involved the kind of 'passive suffering' that Yeats had warned was not a proper subject for artistic treatment. The 'so what' story and the 'too bad' story tended to merge. 'A young man falls in love with a girl and she is unfaithful to him. He is heartbroken.' So? Pity. No story. Did themes actually exist?

And then O'Connor would come to the aid of the class's imagination. 'Or there's that beautiful story by Turgenev,' he would say. 'The one about the young girl who is dying and falls in love with the middle-aged district doctor so that at least she will have been in love before she dies.' And hearing that simple and lovely theme, the class would know that they did exist, although it would by then be quite clear that not everyone would ever have the good fortune and understanding to find one.

In the novel O'Connor sees the *passage* of time as the central ingredient. He abhorred the use of flash-backs in the novel precisely because he felt they disturbed the chronological flow that was the novelist's greatest asset. In the short story, however, there is no such flow and, indeed, there must not be such a flow. The writer is constantly fighting the rhythm of Time, saving everything for a single blinding moment when literally everything that is of importance in the short story happens. The crisis, as he sometimes put it, is not the *culmination* of the short story (as it is of the novel); it *is* the short story.

O'Connor's classes did not, as I have said, have to cope with the problem in this abstract way. All they had to do was to produce the themes themselves. *All* they had to do! And yet the students did come through, and, when they did, a great part of the reward was the reaction of O'Connor himself. 'I could write that story,' he would say. 'I envy you that story.' And suddenly even the most improbable of his students would be able to see a faint line extending all the way from himself to the greatest glories of literature. What had been a private, almost despairing act became for that student at that moment an exciting reality.

III

Of course, the search for themes was not all of it. If the first third or half of an O'Connor writing course was spent in discovering what he wanted in those bedeviling 'four lines', the rest of the course was spent in trying to figure out what to do with them once they were there. O'Connor's advice on this matter was that of the extraordinarily dedicated craftsman who did not hesitate to re-write his own stories dozens of times, who almost never transferred a story from magazine to book or from book to 'collected' book without trying out at least half a dozen new versions of it. His classes, in sum, were in the presence of one of the truly disciplined artists of the twentieth century and his advice was enormously relevant, informed and wise.

One point, for example, had to do with doing a 'treatment' of a story before beginning the actual writing – a 'treatment' being a very rough draft or sketch of the story. Later in life he expressed some doubt that this approach would always be valid, but at the time he was giving his writing courses he felt that most students would benefit from getting 'black on white' as quickly as possible and in a sufficiently flexible form so that they could recast not just the words of the story but its over-all structure. This, of course, is an extension of the theme concept in that it is an attempt to be as sure as possible that one has a properly conceived story before committing one's best writing to it. The problem with the method is that by the time the letting go is to occur the basic impulse may already have been spent. O'Connor himself was remarkable in his ability to retain freshness through numberless versions of a particular story. But even he did not always proceed in this well-organized way. Some stories he wrote down 'just as they came into [his] head'. Other stories started out one way and ended another way. Some stood up on their hind legs and 'told [him] to go to hell'. What O'Connor was really doing with the notion of the 'treatment' was giving his students some sense of how to proceed when the impulse governing the story was not so powerful as to sweep everything before it. How does one go about writing not even on a bad day but on an average sort of day? The answer, in effect, was: try out a rough sketch of the thing and see how it goes. Also, he would sometimes add, it did no harm to listen to a little Mozart first to get in the mood.

Another piece of advice he often gave his students was 'not to skimp on the crisis of the story'. This is an even more direct extension of the theme idea for the theme *is* the crisis and the crisis *is* the story. In practical terms, however, it proved to be a point that had to be stressed independently, and often. His students had a tendency to write through the crisis of a story at the same tempo and pace that they wrote through the rest of the story. In O'Connor's view this was bad construction. What preceded the moment of crisis should, on his view, be told as quickly and expeditiously as possible, conveying necessary information (the information mustn't be left out and O'Connor often criticized Maupassant and Hemingway for failing to get the necessary information in), but always with the idea of moving on towards the crucial moment. When this moment arrived, however, then it must be given its full due. It must not simply state, it must prove the point, and this not intellectually but emotionally.

Directly related was O'Connor's view about the importance of keeping a quite sharp separation between narrative and drama in the writing of a short story. He himself admitted to a tendency to mix the two forms of expression, and most of his students did it frequently. But he stressed that the two had quite different purposes: narrative to state the point and drama to prove it. The great moment for proving points in a short story is characteristically the crisis and, consequently, he liked his crisis as free of interference as possible. A minimum of he says and she says were necessary to keep order, but, after that, the purer the drama the better.

His views on narrative were quite interesting. If the crisis was given over to conversation and action, he felt that the beginning of the story should almost invariably be straight narrative. When a student began his story with a conversation in progress, O'Connor would usually find some fault with it. 'I've tried the "Damn"-said-the-duchess opening,' he would say, 'and it usually doesn't work.' He not only thought the story should characteristically begin with narrative, but, more shockingly, he urged that the tone of the narrative be kept rather pedestrian and factual. 'Prosaic' was, for O'Connor, a term of praise when it came to the opening of a short story. He criticized many of his own earlier stories for being too poetic in the narrative. Or, as he put it in *The Lonely Voice*, there are times when writing should be served up 'cold'. The crisis must be 'piping hot', but the narrative should be cool, a bit like a documentary.

These various points actually fit together and, in conjunction with the theme idea, form a surprisingly coherent view of what is after all an extraordinarily complicated subject. Indeed, O'Connor was able to create in the imaginations of his students a kind of ideal concept of the short story. This story begins in a rather prosaic vein, describing everyday characters doing rather every-

day things, and moves with controlled speed through the necessary dramatic scenes until finally it reaches the crisis – the critical
moment in time that *is* the story – and then the drama and poetry
and emotion break through and the whole landscape of life is lit
up with an eerie and unearthly light. After control and self-
discipline and awareness and intelligence have done their work,
the whole performance dissolves into mystery.

The Young Librarian

DERMOT FOLEY

'Formidable' is the only word to describe him when in 1929 we met for the first time in the Pembroke library, Ballsbridge. He was twenty-six, and had recently moved up from Cork as librarian. I was his deputy. About three years before, I had seen him at a gathering of library people from the provinces. The head I could never have forgotten; the mass of it, the domination in brow and eye. Nor that voice – it seemed to come up from the bowels of the earth.

I came a cropper from the start. Everything I did was wrong and misery stared me in the face for weeks. The abrupt manner was upsetting, so was the suspicion in the watchful eyes. And he shouted. For me there was no enchantment about that trombone blasting into my face. All I wanted was simple answers. There were only two of us at first, and into the empty rooms he would sweep like a gale, leaving in his wake a malediction on invoices, the typewriter, the slovenly charwoman. Or he would reach for the hat after a flaming row over the telephone with a bookseller, maybe, and tear into town to give the man another scalding. It was a blessed relief to be alone, to watch the happy seagulls floating over the river Dodder across the road, and think about this raven I was caged with; the mop of unruly hair, the smear for a moustache, the whipcord suit – all black as jet. Even the pen was black, a huge Parker that looked clumsy in those fastidious fingers. Was this the raw recruit from Cork I had been told about in the city, the librarian half-trained by Lennox Robinson and Geoffrey

Phibbs in primitive county libraries? They said, too, that he was a class of a writer into the bargain.

No war of adjustment is without its discoveries, and I discovered in time that the raging eyes and roaring voice concealed a shy and even inexperienced man with unexpected streaks of gentleness. But meanwhile there was that tempestuous energy with its capacity for exploding in several directions at once. One spouted invective of quite staggering ingenuity, while another carried a salvo that either transformed the problem in an instant, or blew it into little bits that no one could put together again. He was bound to give tongue when cataloguing books, lashing into the bonehead whose masterpiece lay before him and pontificating on the subject, no matter what that was. Like any captive in my position, I always agreed with him, but I had few illusions about this new breed of librarian who bore all the marks of omniscience and pushed aside the registers while he made a meal of any book that took his fancy. It was plain, of course, that the library would never be ready for opening at this gait of going, and that O'Donovan the librarian knew as much about the skills of librarianship as I did about Rainer Maria Rilke, who at that hour of our lives haunted the imagination of O'Connor the poet.

Those weeks of anarchy were like a year, and to continue enduring them did not seem possible. He was so extravagantly intelligent, so hilariously heretical, that I foresaw every rational argument for getting the library in order consigned to the flames at the first syllable. To make matters worse, that voice could hypnotise me. At any moment it might erupt into folk-song or bawdy ballad and shiver the rooms with the vibrations of silver trumpets.

I could never recall afterwards when or how the change in our relations came about. Perhaps he had been in the grip of worries of some kind, causing what he used to call gastritis. He cannot have known, I think, the ordeal I was going through. At any rate, the tension eased, and so did resistance to the methods and organisation I had persisted in introducing. He gave me a book or two to read and walked with me part of the way home of an evening, when he would talk mostly about Cork, and I would listen in silence to the ceaseless flow of it. Then one afternoon he announced out of the blue that he was going to Paris – it was, I think, the time he called to see James Joyce – and where the blazes could he buy a pair of tennis shoes. I produced my own the next morning, and that evening watched him wear them as he walked down the pier at Dun Laoghaire to the mail-boat. All he possessed was an attaché case, a raincoat and a walking-stick; and with the artist's black hat daringly cocked, he headed for Europe.

After that my life was turned towards him and the job, and to nothing else. I was, of course, dominated by his personality and the powerful intellect, but that was not the whole explanation. For one thing, I was drawn by his extraordinary vulnerability and innocence, either of which could lead him into the silliest situations and leave him badly bruised. I remember one occasion when, against all warning, he remonstrated with a young brat who was hitting a tinker-woman on Clyde Road. The fellow turned on Michael like a dog, but before he could raise the fist, my fingers were round his throat. We got rid of them. But Michael, shivering with excitement, began to chastise me for taking such a risk. I hardly heard a word he said, for I was aghast at the horror of his being struck, and at the particular instinct that roused me to his defence. From that moment onwards, I could see ever more clearly that this very formidable-looking man, who had unwittingly caused me so much misery, had a core of such sensitivity and tenderness, that protecting him from boors with a flair for exposing his fragility became a compulsion.

In his company I was lifted out of common-place adolescence to contemplate an entirely new world. He too was growing up and feeling his way in the big city, but in the manner of a young bull escaped from a field. Until I knew him better, it was always embarrassing to see him stopped in the street by someone who had read an article of his in the *Irish Statesman* and believed he might have something to say. Indeed he had, and usually it was delivered with calculated arrogance and pomp. In public conversation he seemed to be hell-bent on annihilating mediocrity, and the innocent as well as the guilty were felled before him.

But this cast-iron confidence in his own opinions was contrary to the impression of insecurity, and suggested that something was out of key. Or was it? I recall a meeting of a small and rather precious discussion-group to which he had been invited. He surprised me by going, and surprised me still more by turning into a pub and swallowing a double whiskey, since he seldom drank at that time. 'Now I can face that lot,' he confided. As it happened, he kicked up a row in his royal manner and walked out, but even that encounter bit deep into him, and it seemed to me that his mission, whatever it was, was going to put him through a torture largely of his own making. In controversy it was plain that few would learn very much about this pilgrim, while many would remember all manner of things about the masks he wore.

Towards the simpler, unpretentious people he was warmth itself. Our postman, despite the rigours of a cottage stuffed with children, was a bird-fancier of some distinction and, along with the morning's mail, delivered curious observations on the hazards of cross-breeding. Michael later visited the poor man many times in hospital. A council plumber returned again and again to repair the lavatory ball-cock, and detecting a malingerer, I was all for reporting him. But I was wasting my time, because Michael was enchanted by the Ringsend accent and the outrageous stories that rogue related about the water systems of gentlewomen on Ailesbury Road.

With AE, Dick Hayes and Osborn Bergin there was neither pomp nor arrogance, nor any sign of a mask. They were, all three, gentle and reserved, and it was unthinkable that a voice should be raised in their company. AE was Michael's point of repose, to whose judgment he deferred as to none other, not even to Yeats, and on the occasions I walked with them, I never

failed to notice the way Michael listened to that remarkable man,
only now and then interjecting something which, when AE
nibbled at it, was seen to be a bait for turning the talk into a new
direction. In the *Irish Statesman* office at Merrion Square one
time, Michael diverted the talk towards music in Ireland, in
which AE showed no interest. Michael's purpose, however, was
to ask if a letter of mine on a state subsidy for opera might be
published. AE would have done virtually anything for the young
Corkman who had blown into Irish writing on a fresh and in-
vigorating wind. I think it was AE who introduced him to Ethel
Montgomery. To her also Michael deferred, but by default, for
her wit enchanted him and his blackest depressions were lifted by
her irrepressible gaiety. 'That's the sort of woman I'd like to
marry – if ever,' he said one Sunday night as we left AE's house,
where she had interrupted the great man's monologue with a peal
of laughter. She was, I suppose, twice his age, but in his staring
adulation she was ageless. With people like these he was safe,
for the time being, from himself. The balance so easily upset by
the fears and insecurity, by the intolerance towards others, was
restored in their company.

Until 1938, when he abandoned librarianship, he was the part-
time writer, but once the Dublin Corporation absorbed the
Pembroke township in 1931, and took the library as well into its
great maw, his interest in the job declined. Up to that he had
enjoyed every moment of it, because we ran the place exactly as
we wished without let or hindrance, even from the pompous old
town clerk. That good man had taken a liking to his librarian,
but expected to be consulted in the proper manner, so that when
he was informed one day of a proposal to acquire a small collection of music scores, for which we ventured to suggest a modest
increase in the book-fund, he hummed and he hawed at this
daring exploitation of the ratepayers, and said he would think
about it. And that, we agreed, was the end of it. A week later
Michael hauled me from the office. 'Get your hat,' he said, the
eyes dancing, 'we're off to Pigott's.' On the tram he showed me a

personal cheque from the town clerk. 'An anonymous cheque, Mr O'Donovan,' quoted Michael, 'for that music'. That sixty-pounds cheque went to our heads, and in no time we had begun a series of gramophone recitals in the children's library, using Michael's gramophone and our common pool of records. We aimed high, playing Haydn and Schubert the first night, only to be bombarded at the close with requests for 'Sonny Boy', which at that date was crucifying the civilised world. However, at the end of two months, a vote on all records played brought Mozart, Haydn, and Schubert to the top, in that order. Our audacity knew no bounds. He proposed, and I seconded, that a small choir be formed, and without more ado children from cottages and mansions assembled on the next half-day, when we had the building to ourselves. At first he took charge, but in the space of ten minutes the children took charge of him, and for a very simple reason. He hated staff notation, in which the sheet was written, and tried to put it to tonic-solfa as he went along, while beating a measure that nobody could follow. Abashed, he flung the book at me, a grudging surrender to my choral training, which he despised. Some discipline having been restored, the children joined with me at the end in inviting him to be the assistant conductor.

Adventurous librarianship of this kind he enjoyed. Book-selection was another pleasure, and not merely because it fed a voracious appetite for reading. He went rampant on continental literature, and to this day the library retains the reputation for it that he made. I tried very hard, however, to keep him out of the lending department, because he interfered as a matter of course with the systems I had devised – not to assert his authority, but, as I saw it, to exercise a residual perversity which said ever so plainly that he was not so impractical as I had successfully proved (he was the most impractical man I ever knew). But it was like keeping the tide back, and time and again I was brought in to resolve confusion caused solely by his own disregard for basic rules of order. He had a habit of moving quietly among the readers, speaking to one or another, and recommending a book to a bewildered wanderer. He kept his eyes open all the time, noting what books were borrowed or left untouched, and who chose them. Back in the office, he often waited like a broody hen, clucking with complaints: the book that someone wanted and was not in the catalogue (my responsibility), or it was that bumpkin of an assistant he saw picking his nose *again*. And that stunning creature with golden hair and the neck of a swan – 'Suffering God, man, you can't have missed her? Pure Botticelli. Go down and find out who she is.'

The number of times he went into raptures over this, that and the other woman were uncountable. Ethel Montgomery, naturally, was a star in his firmament. And Meriel Moore so unbalanced him that he contrived to get a small part opposite her in a silly one-acter at the Peacock. For that I had to rake up a dress suit, pour him into it, and stand in the wings to make up the tie he kept unknotting from sheer fright. Then there was the girl with the aristocratic nose and satin skin – a Brünhilde if ever he saw one – who sat the examination for library assistant. She failed, God be praised, to get the job, and became instead a reader at the library, to which, I suspect, he had invited her. Hearing from me that she had taken out her first book, he rushed down to the counter to see what it was, and boy, oh boy, it was a heart-throb by Berta Ruck. He threw her wretched ticket on the counter in disgust. 'Tell me,' I said one morning, worn out as I was listening to a litany of superlatives about someone else, 'this peach you met last night. What would you do with her anyway?' But he intoned: 'Ah penny, brown penny, brown penny, I am looped in the loops of her hair.' 'Come off it,' I retorted. 'You wouldn't have the guts to kiss her.' 'Who the hell said anything about kissing?' he snorted, and banged the door.

No matter how moody he was when I called at the flat, I could manage most times to dispel it by asking if we might have some music. His records were few, but superb, and it was music of a kind that I, accustomed to grand opera, had only heard about. I cannot listen to Mozart now but I am brought back to that room of spare furniture, the dying fire and darkness about us. It was here that I really found music, and through one whose feeling for it seemed to make nonsense of all the theories I had learned. He had little interest in opera, except for Wagner, whom he tired of in the end, and Mozart. Mozart was unimpeachable in everything he wrote, and whenever I heard one of the arias ringing through the library in his bass voice, I would know that Michael was on the top of his form. His indifference to Palestrina and Victoria, whom I introduced, was explained by what he called his revulsion to church music; but that was an evasion, I think, for he later succumbed to small doses of Bach, a surrender I remember very well, because around the same time he went off to London on a week's leave to hear the Toscanini series of Beethoven symphonies. Another outing – and this time I went along – took the form of a sixteen-mile walk from Rathfarnham and over the mountains into Enniskerry, where we were just able to crawl into a bus and reach the Theatre Royal for a concert by John Sullivan, Joyce's Irish tenor from the Paris Opera. We went quite wild with joy that night.

Michael had the eagerness of a boy and was prepared to try anything when the fit took him. I thought he was joking one day when he said he had bought a couple of dance records, and would I, under pain of excommunication, be at the flat early. It was a disastrous evening. The carpet was rolled back, and there was Mary Manning holding a hopping Michael. 'Get that fellow on the floor,' he bawled without introducing me, 'until I see if he can do it any better.' That wasn't very difficult. He insisted on looking down at his unbiddable feet, and he scowled and giggled and dithered as he hacked away at Mary's ankles and finally tripped over them. Dancing was discarded from that evening. Then he tried tennis, and that too was a disaster. Naturally it was my fault once more, because I kept explaining that the limit lines had a purpose when I should be co-operating like a gentleman by sending the ball back to him with a decent bounce in it, no matter

E

from what point in Herbert Park he had clouted it. After three sessions I gave up, and tennis too was abandoned.

I think he had about seven flats in Dublin before leaving it in 1938. Chelmsford Road was the first. Later, as he acquired more friends, he felt the need for something more commodious, more appropriate to a growing reputation. An even more compelling reason was a fixation about bringing his mother up from Cork. Having settled on rooms at 'Trenton', a fine residence set back among trees opposite the Town Hall at Ballsbridge, he had the problem of furnishing them. He fancied oak, but knew nothing at all about joinery or the fake finishes that abounded in those days; so I, the son of a carpenter, was hauled off to town as adviser. I must say he put on a first-class show: a customer of austere countenance and reflection, who kept passing a hand over table or chair like a professional, showing more interest in the style of it than in the price, while I, at his sly nod, was on my knees making my inspection. Out in the street once more, he relaxed. 'You know, Der,' he said, 'I've always wanted to furnish my own house.' I guessed that paying for it, in cash, counted for as much. The following day I was ordered to drop everything at the library and join him at 'Trenton' for the delivery van. All he was concerned with after the men left was the area around the hearth, and this he enclosed with the leather suite, placing bookshelves at one side of the fire and the gramophone at the other, on the floor. The pattern of the writer at home was unfolding. Meanwhile I had fixed the dining-table and chairs and put down the carpet. Before returning to the library, I poked a nose into the kitchen, and saw that, barring the sink and a wall cupboard not much bigger than a bird-cage, it was bare as a cell; no table, no cups for his guests, and nothing to make even his own breakfast. I ventured to remind him. He waxed authoritarian and handed me a pound note. 'See what you can get for that.'

I know no one who flogged himself at his work as he did. There were no half measures, and no approaching him while he was hammering the thing into shape. On he went, chain-smoking, tense as a tiger. No wonder he often got ill from it. But once he fixed a chapter to his satisfaction, what he wanted most was to read it aloud to someone. He liked to share his joys. The morning he showed me the letter of acceptance from the *Atlantic Monthly* for that marvellous story, 'Guests of the Nation', we danced around the office, and on the expectation of the cheque that was offered (it was, I think, about one hundred and forty dollars), we cleared off to Glendalough for a week-end of rambling and climbing mountains. But at breakfast on the Monday we counted the money we had, and it was not enough to meet the bill. Undaunted, I took the next bus to Dublin, borrowed a few pounds from a friend of his and wired it to him. It arrived, he later told me with a chuckle, while he was enjoying a superb lunch.

For one who lived at an altitude of thinking far above most, Michael was the simplest and kindest of men, showing an unexpected patience in matters that, to him, were important. Like AE, he would devote any amount of time towards helping anyone in whom he detected even a small talent for writing. He imagined that I had a spark of it. The manuscript of my first attempt at a story remains a precious possession; a masterpiece of brutal correction, priceless advice and outrageous humour. It was, in its way, an extension of those happy strolls along the quiet roads around Ballsbridge of an evening, when, listening to him, English became for me a new language, precise and clean. The same revelation had occurred with music, as it would in time with poetry. On one of those nights he stopped suddenly under a tree, the light from the gas-lamp above pouring down through it. 'My God,' he exclaimed, 'how light transforms. How can one possibly describe light? Chekhov says, simply, "The sun was setting." And that's all.' In a book on architecture I had been reading, gothic was defined as 'the dematerialisation of line', and somewhat shyly I mentioned it to him. He stopped dead. 'Marvellous!' he cried. 'Where did you get that?'

In 1931, on being appointed librarian for Clare, I left

Pembroke. Within the previous year the Pembroke township had been absorbed into Dublin city, and it had become plain to us that the Dublin Corporation's bureaucratic notions of running a library would never mix with ours. Michael too had ideas about getting out for a career in writing, but he could not afford it just then. My own fears about facing Clare he dismissed with characteristic mockery. Our parting celebration was tea and buns at Roberts's cafe. 'I suppose,' he said, 'you'll marry a pub. But there are other ways of keeping me supplied with stories.'

Clare was tough and lonely, and I was in no humour to appreciate his first letter which had his drawing of an archangel laying a wreath on my tombstone. I saw him next when I went to Dublin to buy books. He had an attack of his gastritis, induced, he explained, by an auditor who insisted on an explanation for every figure, and by the library staff, which had gone plumb to hell. He turned up in Ennis nearly a year later saying he wanted to see a bit of Clare, so we hired a car and belted round the Burren and the Feakle country. But the wild splendours of Clare seemed only to add to his restlessness, and he poured out complaints about a recent story that had nearly killed him, and the fool he was ever to have taken up writing in the first place. We agreed to meet in Cork for a library conference. 'I want the mother to meet you,' he said, 'but you'll have to put up with it if the Da insists on welcoming you at the station.'

All my doubts about the relationship between us, and what, if anything, it meant to him, were revived by those words, and not until I sat in the tiny cottage at Harrington Square at Cork, watching his mother's adoration and his gentleness towards her, that an answer came. I recalled things I had forgotten, like his saying one time that he and I could make a success of sharing his flat. And he had once boiled up with excitement on the idea that we could set up a bookshop together, where writers could assemble and talk in a poets' den at the back. It now seemed to me that what he desperately needed was companionship; companionship and a chopping block, the two requirements that the average man finds in marriage. But he was no average man. For the first time I saw the loneliness.

After Cork there was the long series of letters that kept my head above water until my own marriage. And Dublin was now a firm date whenever I could get there. Sometimes he could not wait, but let himself go over the telephone, or sent a telegram with the terse words: 'Come up.' I might find him in foul humour flaking at the typewriter, or stretched on the bed sick with exhaustion. One day he looked so distressed that I dragged him out, and for want of somewhere better to go, headed for the Central Criminal Court. The galleries were jammed with onlookers, but no one appeared to have any interest in the little woman with the shawl in the dock, charged with poisoning her husband. A barrister whom Michael knew came across to us at the adjournment, and with cheerful detachment tried to soothe Michael's compassionate questions with the remark: 'Oh, she'll get off. Poisoners usually do, you know.' In a café downtown we talked for an hour about the life that lay before her if she were acquitted, as we hoped she would be, and before we reached the flat his temperature was back to normal. But it was to shoot up again once I had gone, and within a week I was sitting with him again, listening to that wonderful story, 'In the Train', which he had wrought from that court scene.

His letters contained a few broadsides on the intrigues and manœuvring at the Abbey Theatre, of which he was now a director. And it was playing merry hell with him. Inevitably his involvement with the theatre tempted him towards writing plays. He learned a lot about the craft from Hugh Hunt, the producer, whose work he admired, but the crudeness of drama as an art form horrified him. 'It's a barbarous form of literature,' he explained. 'You can't suggest anything, as in a short story. You have to shout it, not once but three times, in case the audience should forget it.' With Hunt's collaboration he wrote three plays, of which *The Invincibles* was for me the most memorable. In the closing scene on the first night, when young Kelly (played by

Cyril Cusack) sang 'Hail, Queen of Heaven' for Joe Brady in the adjacent condemned cell, we were both so moved that we took it up, and in a moment the entire audience was singing.

Before his marriage he at last threw up his job in Pembroke, and rented a fine house in Woodenbridge, Co. Wicklow. 'Lynduff' was beautifully sited in that valley, and he was to find that the open air and the regularity of the life would improve his health. He worked much better too, and was by now doing occasional talks for the B.B.C. I accompanied him to London for the very first broadcast of his Irish poetry translations. Well before the scheduled time, around eleven at night, we were there waiting, and a more jittery Michael I had seldom seen. As he was about to enter the studio, a young man with alarm in his face burst into the room jabbering something about a hitch and an important announcement. Poor Michael almost crumpled at the knees. We waited, and then over the speaker beside us came the dramatic news that Chamberlain was returning unexpectedly from his meeting with Hitler at Munich. I shall never forget his anguish as that official returned to take him to the studio, leaving me to hear a stunned nation being told that Frank O'Connor would now read some medieval Irish verses.

Looking back, that night in 1938 is for me a fateful turning-point in Michael's life, a prelude to adversity stretching out to the early 1950s and the first lectures in America. He was thirty-five, and just commencing his writing career, when war came to dry up nearly all those sources of income that keep the struggling writer going, only he now had wife and family to support. But there was worse than war. That nervous temperament of his, which under normal conditions manufactured one crisis after another out of trifle or tragedy, put him to the limit of tension. For every page he wrote he must have destroyed fifty. A few of his books were outlawed by the state, and others were excluded from the libraries by the parish guardians of morality. But he never surrendered. There was at least one humane editor to be found in Ireland, and he accepted a weekly article (published under an assumed name) for the *Sunday Independent*, a kindness Michael was never to forget.

I still wonder at the iron will and rigorous dedication that brought him through the desolation to produce the stories and translations, the lectures, the memorable broadcasts. And after all that he could put away the hurt and the bitterness and come back mellowed and refreshed to live out his days in the Ireland he loved so passionately; this exasperating Ireland that always, it seems, will be ashamed of the writer who dares to crumble the crust of appearances in order to discover the reality beneath.

It is impossible to remain unmoved by the courage of the writer to whom all antagonisms raised between him and his objective are challenges to be taken up. And when the man within the writer manages to the very end to preserve his personal integrity, we who have known him can only slink away to meditate on our own weaknesses, and on the mess we make of our own challenges.

Frank O'Connor and the Irish Theatre

ROGER McHUGH

> Yeats wanted new, young blood on the Board of Directors and so F. R. Higgins was appointed a Director in April 1935, Frank O'Connor in the following October and Ernest Blythe joined the Board in the same year. Frank O'Connor resigned in 1939 and Higgins died in 1941. Higgins had been Managing Director and after his death Ernest Blythe took his post.
>
> LENNOX ROBINSON, *Ireland's Abbey Theatre*

Yeats, as usual, knew what he was about in artistic matters, even in old age. Higgins had proved himself as a poet and soon turned his attention to the theatre with *A Deuce of Jacks* (September 1935). O'Connor had written poetry and short stories of quality. One of the best known of his stories, 'In the Train', was dramatised and produced by Hugh Hunt (31 May 1937), and its success probably encouraged O'Connor to collaborate with Hunt in two plays, *The Invincibles* (18 October 1937) and *Moses' Rock* (25 February 1938). Years afterwards, in a series of articles first published in *The Bell*, later in separate form as *The Art of the Theatre* (1947), O'Connor indicated some of the advantages of collaboration which he had gleaned from experience. One was that of being able to use the theatre as a workshop in which practitioners of several crafts can work together. The theatre of the Elizabethans, of Molière and of the early Abbey period had known this kind of collaboration; and indeed the appointment of O'Connor and of Higgins (Ernest Blythe was nominated by the state) now seems part of Yeats's plan to restore it, for about the same time the services of Hugh Hunt and of the designer Tanya Moiseiwitsch had been enlisted by him.

The other relevant advantage which O'Connor mentions is that of learning by practical experience the difference between the art of the story-teller which, through the availability of books, has become accommodated to the solitary reader, and the public art of drama, whose practitioners must have a sense of community and of communication, so that the play becomes a shared game, the playwright using to the full extent the unique sounding-board which an audience provides. Almost all O'Connor's writing has a strong dramatic quality; both Hunt's dramatisation of 'In the Train' and Neil McKenzie's of 'Guests of the Nation' (1960) realise that quality which underlies the lyrical impressionism of his stories. It is to be seen also in the power of some of his early poems in the dramatic mode, 'The Patriot', 'Echoes' and others, some of them translations of Irish lyrics:

> Patrick, you chatter too loud
> And lift your crozier too high,
> Your stick would be kindling, soon,
> If my son Osgar were by. . . .

There was indeed a strong self-dramatising element in his own personality, evident in his personal bearing, his gesture and speech, his active likes and dislikes. Also, the narrator's art, as a famous monologue by Stephen Dedalus emphasises, is half-way to being that of the dramatist, since an audience is postulated. But O'Connor's close contact with the theatre gave him a chance denied to or missed by the author of that ingrown play, *Exiles*; and he used it to realise in some measure one of his potentialities.

The Invincibles and *Moses' Rock* are both plays about Irish historical events and show a certain logical progression in that the first dramatises a series of actual happenings and characters, while the second imagines something which might have happened to a family living during a critical period of history.

The Invincibles concerns the group of men known by that name who in 1882 assassinated the new Chief Secretary for Ireland, Sir Frederick Cavendish, and the Irish Under-Secretary, Thomas Burke, in Phoenix Park. This action was planned as a reprisal against a British policy of coercion and eviction by men who believed that it would prove effective where political action had proved inept. The 'Park Murders' were followed by the betrayal of Joe Brady, Timothy Kelly and other Invincibles by James Carey, who had been a member of their council and who cracked under the special attention of Inspector Mallon. Carey turned Queen's evidence; his former comrades were hanged.

This is a theme which presents an obvious problem of characterisation; those involved in the assassination were desperate men who, failing to reach the chief target of anti-eviction hostility, the Chief Secretary, 'Buckshot' Forster, murdered his replacement, the innocent and well-disposed Cavendish, as well as the undoubtedly culpable Burke. Their action was condemned by Parnell, who wished to free his campaign from any suggestion of implication (the famous *Times* forgeries later attempted to manufacture proof of it) and it undoubtedly shocked the Irish people as a whole. Further, Carey (who was shot later on his way to Australia) passed into Irish history as the worst kind of informer. If the deed was wholly black and Carey merely a shade blacker, a certain monotony of dramatic colour was unavoidable. If, on the other hand, the popular sympathy for Brady and his companions displayed at the time of their executions was merely an application of national whitewash to the victims of an informer, a dramatist of integrity could not pretend that it was anything else or use it as a convenient colour-contrast.

O'Connor tried to get behind the stereotype to the individual: Brady and Kelly, he found, appeared from the evidence to be simple men, tired of the posturing which marked post-Fenian patriotism, suspicious of party politicians who seemed to them to have submitted tamely to the arrest of Parnell; in the words of the Dublin street-ballad, England had 'locked the pride of Erin's isle into dark Kilmainham Jail' without a hand being raised against her. Further, the Invincibles were stung to precipitate action by the police massacre of a number of children who refused to disperse when celebrating Parnell's release. Carey, on the other hand, was no frightened renegade; he was a substantial builder who had something to lose by joining the Invincibles; he was both scared enough and had sense enough to see that Cavendish's appointment might produce a new climate of opinion and tried to save him from sharing Burke's fate. But he did not crack easily; he was true to his companions despite the financial ruin caused by his arrest, until Mallon carefully stage-managed a succession of 'scenes' near his cell which convinced him that one of his comrades had informed on him; then he moved to get his confession in first.

By holding a balance between altruism and opportunism in his characterisation of Carey and between a rugged, desperate patriotism and the ordinary effects of guilt in Brady and Kelly, O'Connor made all three characters credible; while, by commencing his play with the absurd wrangle between the 'Denzille Street Fenians' and the 'Peter Street Fenians', who spend most of their time sentencing each other to death, he made their desperation understandable. 'History will be made for the future not by armies, but by a handful of determined men,' says Carey; to Kelly and the rest the removal of Burke is nothing beside the deaths caused by police brutality and eviction. The first act is a good study of precipitate action set against blathering ineptitude and political disillusionment. The second shows men labouring not only under the stress of guilt and fear but under the burden of knowing that the people for whom they struck are united with the blatherers and the politicians in their condemnation. The final scenes make good use of Mallon's ingenuity in tricking Carey and of the confrontation of the condemned Joe Brady by the sister of the slain Burke, a nun who urges him to ask forgiveness for the one deed of his life for which he does not want to be forgiven. Traditionally, Brady walked to the scaffold murmuring, 'Poor oul' Ireland, poor oul' Ireland', while Carey, conscious of

Mallon's deception, aware of the hate mounting against him and knowing that he was doomed to exile, shouted, 'Hang me with them!' If O'Connor did not completely avoid melodrama, it was not absent from his material. Tim Kelly, a choir-boy in Clarendon Street church, really sang 'The Heart Bowed Down' to console Brady the night before they both died. And, to extend the argument for a moment outside the play, Brady's mother, who in the play is represented as telling her son 'to take his secrets to the grave', years later would point to the coat he wore on that fatal afternoon in the Phoenix Park and would say to her visitors, '*That's* the coat he done it in!'

Joe Brady's last speeches provide a link with O'Connor's next play. 'God's curse on them, why don't they fight, if 'twas only with their bare fists!' Brady says of the people, anticipating a more famous rebuke to the same effect: 'Like that crawling reptile, Carey, Ireland ran away from the names they put on her and went whinging to her prayers. But one day, mark you, she'll do the same thing to Parnell, and then he'll know what we went through in the long nights at Kilmainham.' *Moses' Rock* is a play about the effects of the Parnellite split upon an imagined small-town Irish family, the O'Learys, and their friends. Historical events – the beginning of the split, its deepening, and the death of Parnell – provide a unifying framework, but the real subject is the changing relationships of the people within it and particularly the development of young Joan O'Leary in relation to her widowed father (a substantial merchant) and three suitors. These are Ned Hegarty, a patriotic journalist, with whom she is romantically in love; Jer Coghlan, a lawyer; and Lieutenant Fortescue, a British army officer stationed in the town.

At the start all is set for the triumph of the first; Hegarty has just been released from his incarceration for the Parnellite cause and is being dined by Cady O'Leary, her father, who is determined that Hegarty shall win both Joan and a seat at Westminster. Hegarty himself is about to propose to her, but learning that his friend Coghlan, who defended him at his trial, is also in love with

her, he cavalierly puts friendship first and defers the matter for
some months. As for Fortescue, his stock is lowest of all; although
a persistent and impassioned suitor, he is British and Britain is still
the chief enemy. Despite the divorce proceedings against him,
Parnell still has the support of the people; 'like a rock', says
Hegarty. 'Moses' rock,' says the family doctor, Jackson; 'And
remember there is always another power bidding for your
democracy when it's on the warpath. Don't forget the Church.'

By the following summer, with the deepening of the split, the
changes have begun. Joan, resenting the honourable relinquish-
ment of Hegarty, is going with Coghlan; Coghlan has turned
anti-Parnellite, for the sake of his practice and through the pressure of his brother, Father Henry; Fortescue is still trying, but is
put out of court by Coghlan's revelation to Joan that his rival has
been involved in a divorce case, like Parnell. But she is beginning
to think for herself about politics and about her father, who is
clearly wavering in his political allegiance. Also she notices a
strange change in her Aunt Kate, who has been as virulent as
Stephen Dedalus's Dante about Parnell's adultery, when Parnell
was still strong, but now is twice as virulent about those who
deserted him. Aunt Kate has remembered her own love for a
Fenian, whose death soured her life, and the second Act closes
with her passionate cry:

> Almighty God, have pity on that poor man. Have pity on our
> poor distracted people! Have pity on me that wasted my life in
> bitterness and don't let the lives of the young be wasted like
> mine!

The third Act takes place on the day after Parnell's funeral and
on the eve of Joan's marriage to Coghlan. The sell-out of Parnell is
reflected in O'Leary's sale of his principles:

> COGHLAN. The sort of candidate we need is a man with influence
> and a good business to his back. A man who's popular.
> There'd be no doubt whatever about his success. The clergy
> will support him to a man, and his only opponents would

be the old Fenians and a sprinkling of wild young men. The people won't dare to oppose the Church.

O'LEARY. Well?

COGHLAN. The only one the Parnellites have is Ned Hegarty.

O'LEARY. You came to make me an offer, you said.

COGHLAN. Would you stand against Hegarty?

O'LEARY. Me?

COGHLAN. Of course, we realise it would be more than a little awkward for you, but there are certain advantages as I think you'll recognise.

O'LEARY. Stand against Ned Hegarty? That's a serious matter, young man. I don't know could I do it, even if I wanted to. Ned is an old friend of mine.

COGHLAN. For the sake of Ireland, Mr O'Leary.

O'LEARY. Oh, yes, of course, Ireland comes first. All my life I've sacrificed everything to the cause of Ireland. Still – if 'twas anyone else except Ned Hegarty. People might say things.

COGHLAN. Remember Ireland, Mr O'Leary.

O'LEARY. Yes, yes, we must never forget old Ireland. I'll tell you what I'll do. I'll talk to Peter Hurley the bandmaster. Anything I do will have to be done in consultation with the band.

O'Leary, who at the start had been bent on marrying Joan to Hegarty and on supporting him for parliament, has now completed a shabby circle of trimming. 'Never contradict your husband,' he says to Joan. 'If he says black is white, you say 'tis white. If he says the earth is flat, say 'tis flat. I'm speaking to you now as if I was your mother.' But Joan also has been changed by the split. Disillusioned by the sudden shabbiness which life has assumed, she elopes with Fortescue. Less predictably, she is swayed to this decision by her puritanical aunt, whom the death of Parnell has forced to face her own conscience and to live up to her protest against wasting the lives of the young.

This is a much more creative play and shows that O'Connor had learned rapidly that the dramatist interested in history has more scope when he is not bound closely to the actual events of history and can use them better as a catalyst than as a splint. The change forces him into proper characterisation and although here some of the characters, notably Hegarty and Fortescue, are not quite convincing, the whiskey-and-watery, amiable, fussy O'Leary, his bitter sister, Kate, the developing Joan and the opportunistic Coghlan are all well drawn and real. It also forces him to write dialogue which is less geared to established fact, less elucidatory and more concerned with creating its own context of situation and of individual character. In *The Art of the Theatre* O'Connor remarks that 'Good dramatic dialogue is never self-contained; it is full of holes', by which he means that it carries implications of character and of situation and action, avoids the literary touch. This might be illustrated well by much of the dialogue of this play:

JOAN. No, no, no. I won't, I won't.

KATE. Won't what?

JOAN. I won't go away with him. He's a notorious bad character. He did terrible things.

KATE. Then why did you keep going with him?

JOAN. I couldn't get rid of him. I wrote to him twenty times breaking it off.

KATE. Once is breaking it off. Twenty times is dragging it on.

JOAN. I don't care. I won't do it. It would break Daddy's heart. It might ruin Jer's career. Once and for all I won't go away with him.

KATE. Now, who asked you to go away with him?

JOAN. What did you ask me then?

KATE. Goodness gracious, is the child deaf? I asked you to go up and say goodbye to him. You kept him trailing after you long enough.

JOAN. I won't, I won't.

KATE. It's so queer you should think I wanted you to run away with him. I wonder now what put that into your head? Such a crazy notion. Run away with him the night before you were married? What would your father say?

JOAN. Aunt Kate, what would he say?

KATE. Oh, he'd say a lot, but that wouldn't worry me. But if you think 'twould break his heart – well, somehow I don't think

it would. I don't really know what your father's heart is
made of, girl, but I wouldn't say 'twas breakable stuff. And
I wouldn't rely on breaking Mr Jer Coghlan's either – or
the irritation in his chest he calls a heart.

There is also a subtle use of minor characters. O'Leary's mother,
old Shivaun, not only sets off her son's pretensions by her simplicity, but, because she is rambling in her mind and racy in her
talk, she also brings back strong racial reminiscences of the
Famine and of the older Gaelic culture whose destruction it
almost completed; while Dr Jackson, a Darwinist and a rationalist,
is a family friend whose integrity helps Joan's development and
whose critical view of politics reaches into the future. Such overtones help the play's perspective and depth.

It is a matter of conjecture why O'Connor began with historical
plays. Technically better dramatists than he, including Shakespeare, have cut their teeth on them, but I think that there were
other reasons. Yeats, somewhere or another, had remarked that
one big need of his time was to provide autobiographies for the
future. History is, in a sense, the autobiography of a nation, and
there was a strong streak of national consciousness in O'Connor,
somewhat like the uncompromising Fenian element which in
John O'Leary appealed so much to Yeats. It is also relevant that he
had himself followed the Fenian line in the Civil War and had
found himself involved in a disastrous political split; the real
issues rapidly disappeared in a Druid mist of documents, from
which eventually Tweedledum and Tweedledee emerged in
possession. The historical play thus may have offered both a
creative challenge and an opportunity for a critical examination of
conscience and of values, involving such questions as violence, the
right of the majority to be wrong, the nature of integrity in
politics, Church involvement in political matters. The impact of
the violence of the Invincibles and of the Parnellite split upon the
Irish people may have provided the necessary objective correlative
for the expression of O'Connor's own experiences.

But of course these plays exist primarily as good plays, and they had some influence on the writers of the war years. The war put a wall around Ireland; outside it was a threat; inside, the sense of being locked into the status quo. I think that some writers of that time turned to the historical play with the feeling that, since we were cast in upon ourselves, there was a chance to assess the past, others perhaps with a proleptic sense of social reform wished to provide some touchstones for whatever new Ireland might emerge from the wreckage. The trouble was that the theatre for which they hoped to write afforded very little in the way of recent models, even bad models. W. R. Fearon's *Parnell of Avondale* (1934) was, I think, the only Abbey historical play of the ten years preceding *The Invincibles*. But Hugh Hunt's production of *Coriolanus* and then of Denis Johnston's adaptation of Toller's *Blind Man's Buff* (1936) had at least shown that new techniques suitable to the historical play could be attempted in a theatre becoming strangled by the three-act realistic-set fourth-wall production appropriate to the prevailing pattern of George Shiels's successes but to little else. The combined talents of Hunt and O'Connor, added to the effect of the much more imaginative Gate Theatre productions, helped to carry matters a stage further by the fluid shifts of time and scene in *The Invincibles* or by the interplay of character within the more conventional framework of *Moses' Rock*. The latter play managed to convey much more about the real impact of Parnell, the real disaster of the split, through a dozen imaginary characters followed through one year than Fearon's thirty characters (mostly authentic) presented through the vicissitudes of a decade. What both plays also demonstrated was that the essential approach is not through history, research and authentic period dialogue, but through the hearts and minds of humans involved in a human dilemma which history has helped to create. I do not think that it was mere coincidence that Mervyn Wall's play about Kevin O'Higgins, Edward Sheehy's *The Dingle Republic*, Padraic Fallon's *The Seventh Step* and others of a similar kind were written about this time. These plays were

F

not produced in the Abbey Theatre; indeed, by the time they were written Frank O'Connor had resigned from its board, and the other melancholy events mentioned by Lennox Robinson in the statement which I have quoted had occurred. Hugh Hunt and Tanya Moiseiwitsch, incidentally, seem to have left about the same time.

Frank O'Connor's last play received its first production not by the Abbey Theatre Company, but by the Dublin Drama League (8 December 1941). Where his previous plays had treated the past with its implications for the future, *The Statue's Daughter* deals with the present and its involvements with the past. This comedy is set in a small Irish town in which a committee of citizens set up a statue to honour the memory of Brian O'Rourke, a dead hero of the War of Independence. Before this memorial is unveiled, rumours that the hero has fathered an illegitimate daughter split the townspeople into factions; certain lay-popes formerly in the van of the movement to erect the statue now do their best to blow it to pieces. They are frustrated by a combination of the older people of O'Rourke's generation and their children, whose latent idealism is forced by the crisis from under the overlay of materialism and cynicism of the new Ireland. The statue thus becomes a focal point for the interplay of two generations, their revaluation of attitudes towards each other and towards the problems of modern Ireland, and their search for a common ground between people of different faiths and traditions.

It would be pleasant to record that this play, which anticipated so much that is happening in Ireland a quarter of a century later, and which is one of only two plays by O'Connor written without a collaborator, is his most successful, but I do not think it is. The strong situation established in the first two Acts nets itself in several minor love-comedies and an ineptly handled comic reversal in the later scenes. The dictum of Yeats which O'Connor echoed, 'Never conceal a secret from your audience', is in fact proved valid as much by the weakness of the last Act as by the strength of the first. The symbolism of the statue that restores idealism in the older generation and quickens it in the new, giving them a common front against the blatherers and the bigots who block their horizons, is somewhat overworked by the end of the play. Yet there are memorable things in it; notably the Statue's Daughter herself. She is Joan Latham, a parson's niece, who had always believed herself the daughter of a British army officer who had deserted his wife before she died. Suddenly another uncle convinces her that she is the illegitimate daughter of Brian O'Rourke, the dead hero; enthusiastically identifying herself with her newly discovered roots, she tries to learn Irish, inclines towards Catholicism, openly proclaims her pride in her father; finally, she has to face the harsh truth that her uncle is a compulsive liar and that she is in fact no bastard at all. Yet her illusion has achieved something; it has led to a confrontation between 'the Holy Joes that tar the trees so that we'll spoil our clothes if we go out for a coort and censor every decent book in the library ... the gang that dress up like the Ku Klux Klan and have grips and passwords like the Freemasons', the patriots who would turn their heroes into plaster saints, and on the other hand the people, young or old, with enough sensitivity and imagination to be stirred by the idea of a finer, more tolerant Ireland. The two old men who forestall the dynamiters by prematurely unveiling the statue do so because her search was once theirs; young Fintan, who had joined the Knights of Columbanus to save the business which his father's generosity 'in the cause' had brought near to ruin, is booted out of that shabby organisation for her sake; and the bridge built by the event between old and young looks like surviving, or so the last scene between Joan and O'Rourke's friend Costello implies:

COSTELLO. Cheer up, Joan. Look at that statue after all the gunpowder that's been wasted on it. I think it probably does mean something after all.

JOAN. I wonder whether anything does mean very much.

COSTELLO. Oh, yes, it does, look at me. I'm very like the statue. I've been blown up so many times, and there are so many chips off me, and yet I'm still here. We live in faith, and

I've kept true to the faith I had as a boy; that life can be a thousand times nobler and finer than anything we imagine. And even if I die and never see anything like my dreams, life will still have been a little bit better just because somebody had them. ... And tonight I'm going to see the statue's daughter home.

I am much deceived if there is not an autobiographical flavour to this farewell speech. O'Connor had an enduring spirit and much faith in the young. Twenty years ago, when some of us protested against the Abbey's declining artistic standards, he publicly supported us, but said that he had no hope that the Abbey could be saved. He said that it was like trying to save a newspaper whose director was obsessed by football and who recruited his staff on the basis of their proficiency as footballers. It is sad, now that the national theatre is showing some signs of life again, that Frank O'Connor is not around to help:

> *This is the candle climbs the stair,*
> *This is the wind blows it about,*
> *This is a sea-gull cries in the air,*
> *'Life is many, is many, is many,*
> *Is fair, fair, fair,'*
> *This is the wind that blows it out.*

[*Note:* The text of *Time's Pocket*, produced at the Abbey in December 1938, was not available to Professor McHugh when writing this essay.]

The Innocence of Frank O'Connor

EAVAN BOLAND

There is an obscure Irish fable which tells the adventures of three
knights who sheltered out of summer rain in a mountain cave one
night; according to the story, they found a woman of wonderful
beauty there who made them very welcome, so much so that by
morning each of them was resolved to have her love. Each one of
them knelt to her and beseeched her to come with them, to share
and improve their fortunes. To the first and second of these
knights she replied strangely: 'Both of you have possessed me,
both of you have lost me.' She turned away from their protests to
the third and youngest of her suitors; to him she was more generous: 'You also have possessed me and at this minute are losing
me. I am Youth and cannot wait with any man; but because by
your beauty and hope you cherished me, I shall mark your head
and from now on every man who catches sight of you will
recognise you as one of mine.' With that she rested her thumb for
a second between his eyes, and for the remainder of his life a small
print on his forehead marked him out from other men.

  Innocence is lost and found in as many ways as men live; this
legend in its outline captures one of the mysteries of this. In the
beginning innocence is mixed with childhood and ignorance as
green leaves are involved with a tree; time and winter blast the
man and strip the tree, then both are reduced to an existence whose
only innocence is nakedness. Slowly some men and some trees
accept a purgatory of growth; they become innocent again and
green again.

This is the design; the details change with every human experience. All one can say as one goes past a great humiliated tree in December is – it will be green again. In the same way there are writers who expose their loss of innocence so that one glimpses the fabled thumbprint between their eyes; then one can say – he will be innocent again.

An Only Child is the story of Michael O'Donovan's youth until he became twenty years of age. The narrative, by devices of irony and by an intense, simple retrospect creates the features of a single boy. The lasting impression is of a head by Rembrandt, where darkness and light have dramatised the face into a parable, and here the parable is of innocence. Each episode is a prism which reflects another aspect of innocence and the ways in which experience, violence and hope itself assaulted it. This perfect chronicle surpasses any of his short stories and a great number of them gather extra power when placed in the light of *An Only Child*. This is not to say that his short stories do not stand by themselves; they do. Nor is it that one wishes to advocate the philistinism of twisting every sentence into a personal reference, but that *An Only Child* throws brightly into relief a drama of disappointment and hope, of innocence and its loss from which Frank O'Connor never escaped. As some men return to and explore the neighbourhoods where they were young, Frank O'Connor goes back to Michael O'Donovan, approaching him now with reverence, now with irony, now attached to him as in 'The Duke's Children', now grotesquely detached as in 'My Oedipus Complex'.

The experiences which are described in *An Only Child* are unique for their wry sadness; at the same time they belong to a community of similar moments in which other men lost innocence and set out to recover it. Seen as a detail in this pattern the encounters of *An Only Child* are not diminished, but take on extra beauty as colours do in daylight.

Innocence preoccupies the heart of a great deal of human

expression, particularly in the case of poets. Poets seek out images, and in retrospect innocence is an image:

> *A pigeon tumbling in clear summer air –*
> *A laughing schoolboy without grief or care*
> *Riding the springy branches of an elm.*

It is principally an image of exuberance before knowledge has started to blight it:

> *We were as twinn'd lambs that did frisk i' th' sun*
> *And bleat the one at th' other: what we changed*
> *Was innocence for innocence; we knew not*
> *The doctrine of ill-doing nor dreamed*
> *That any did.*

These are the expressions which Keats and Shakespeare gave to an innocence with which all life begins; the beauty of it is inseparable from a fatal trust in its own impressions, and these are as unsafe as dew, as easily burned away. Yeats in his *Autobiographies* describes the childish visions of this innocence: 'Once I smelled new-mown hay when we were quite a long way from land and once when I was watching the sea parrots I noticed they had different ways of tucking their heads under their wings, or I fancied it, and said to the captain "they have different characters".' In 'My Oedipus Complex' Frank O'Connor gives another voice to this impermanent delight: 'I always woke with the first light and with all the responsibilities of the previous day melted, feeling myself rather like the sun, ready to illumine and rejoice.' With irony as bitter as a lemon 'My Oedipus Complex' tells a droll, tough story about how this joy was shattered into a joyless cunning. But even when this process is complete, when the reversal of innocence has been accomplished, the image of a boy beginning his day in imitation of the sun rises out of the action like a flare over a shipwreck.

The type of innocence which Frank O'Connor describes in 'My Oedipus Complex' is that of Blake's rose; an invisible worm has found it out and its destruction is inevitable from the beginning: 'The innocent and the beautiful have no enemy but time.' Of itself this would give a brilliant aspect to *An Only Child*; but the obstacles Michael O'Donovan encounters there wreck an innocence at once greater and more complicated than any which is smashed in 'My Oedipus Complex'. There, the individual prejudices and illusions of a child run aground; but in *An Only Child* it is not simply this which is at stake, but a collective innocence, an innocence of history.

To distinguish between the two one might say that a man approaches his life with a double vulnerability. He has first of all, like the child in 'My Oedipus Complex', the separate wishes of his heart to consider; when these are betrayed he loses one kind of innocence. However, it can happen that over and above this, some men are circumscribed by energies at once more innocent and more vulnerable than any which are purely personal. These are the intangible forces of history which fashion in some men an awareness which cannot be satisfied by anything short of a radiant intuition about identity.

The two generous sources of identity are love and history. In 'My Oedipus Complex' the child's innocence is lost in a confusion about his own meaning to his mother, because her love, which he has relied on, appears to be replaced by love for her husband: 'As time went on I saw more and more how he managed to alienate mother and me. What made it worse was that I couldn't grasp his method or see what attraction he had for mother. In every possible way he was less winning than I.'

But the identity which Michael O'Donovan seeks for in *An Only Child* cannot be supplied or lost as easily as this. Born to privation, he begins to search for a bounty at first vaguely defined by those 'who wore boots and got education', for a correlative of his famished imagination. This is not a unique search; all over the world intelligent, dissatisfied men are employed on it. But in Michael O'Donovan's case there was a peculiar innocence, a special need for identity, special assaults upon that innocence and reasons for that need which can only be understood in terms of Ireland and her history.

History cannot be generous in supplying the meaning of an individual until it has supplied the meaning of a nation. Across years of humiliation no people can hold their possessions intact and least of all their chief possession of identity. Sooner or later they begin to lose it by seeing themselves through the eyes of their oppressors, and to measure worth by that measure until pride becomes shame, self-knowledge self-denial. Yet a people who take so long to form, like a rock in the sun, cannot altogether be destroyed; like a human soul, once they are created they exist.

When a country's meaning is scattered like casually distributed clues in a paper-chase – as Ireland's had been by the turn of this century – a bittersweet phenomenon occurs. Certain men, born into haphazard and incoherent surroundings, do not acquiesce to them, but grow isolated. For a while they search dispiritedly for a contrast, until one day they stumble on a clue in the paper-chase. In their attempt to follow it out, to reconcile it with the blind alleys of their previous experience, a huge and tragic innocence is involved.

Frank O'Connor shares with James Joyce and Patrick Kavanagh the ambiguous luck of such a discovery. In *An Only Child* he details his isolation from his environment; he draws away from the debased outlook of his father's family in favour of the gay independence of his mother. He describes his childish revulsion against his father's mother: 'when I glanced into the kitchen and saw Grandmother at one of her modest repasts – a mess of hake and potatoes boiled in a big pot, with the unpeeled potatoes afterwards tossed on the table to be dipped in a mound of salt and eaten out of the fingers, and a jug of porter beside these – I fled for very shame.' This is something more than a child's fastidiousness; it is a choice in the direction of self-respect, a movement away from the humiliation of centuries. 'One of the things I have inherited from my mother's side of the family is a passion for gaiety. I do not have it myself – I seem to take more after my father's family which was brooding, melancholy and violent – but I love gay people and books and music.'

The ways by which Michael O'Donovan intensified his isolation and escaped into an imaginative kingdom where he could pursue his own identity were circuitous. For a start, he discovered boys' school stories for the contrast their elegance and privilege (albeit pastiche) provided to his own circumstances: 'Their appeal to me was that the characters in them were getting a really good education and that some of it was bound to brush off on me.' This moment of childish insecurity has something in common with the sensation Joyce describes in *A Portrait* when, as a child, he is accompanying his father through Cork and suddenly feels the reality of his childhood perishing in his mind. 'He had not died but he had faded out like a film in the sun. He had been lost or had wandered out of existence, for he no longer existed. How strange to think of him passing out of existence in such a way, not by death, but by fading out in the sun or by being lost and forgotten somewhere in the universe.'

In *An Only Child* Michael O'Donovan's innocence is threatened just because his existence contradicts the evidence of the world around him. He is tenacious of his misfit soul, determined to preserve its hostile reality intact against the sort of dissolution Joyce experiences for that second in *A Portrait*. At first he finds the only way to do so is to inhabit another world, to soar out of his confinement and towards it, like a bird. When he joins the Great Western Railway as a messenger boy, the insult this drudgery delivers to his burgeoning mind makes him retreat still further. He describes himself as living 'a life so divided against itself that it comes back to me now as a hallucination rather than as a memory'.

Another extremely moving version of this attempt to discover an identity confused by environment is in 'The Duke's Children'. This story describes the resentment and isolation which must precede the making of any sensibility. The story is about a boy born into wretched circumstances, just as Michael O'Donovan was – and of course many of the details correspond exactly to those of *An Only Child* – who defends himself by creating a larger meaning for himself. 'Though I might be for the moment at least, only a messenger, I had those long spells when by some sort of instinct I knew who I really was, could stand aside and watch myself coming up the road after my day's work with relaxed and measured steps, turning my head slowly to greet some neighbour with a grace and charm that came of centuries of breeding.' He comforts himself by suspecting that he is a changeling – and, in the broader sense, Michael O'Donovan was: 'In those moments of blinding illumination when I was alone in the station yard on a spring morning with sunlight striking the cliffs above the tunnel, I realized that it was not for long, that I was a duke or earl, lost, stolen or strayed and that I had only to be discovered for everything to fall into its place.'

Any connection between these subterfuges of the imagination and innocence may at first seem to be contrived; but not when one considers that innocence is sheltered by illusion and wrecked by disillusion. Coming to consciousness in an incoherent society, Michael O'Donovan found himself to be a changeling. Like Patrick Kavanagh in a northern agricultural community, or Joyce among the superstitions of the Dublin middle class, Michael O'Donovan's imagination demanded a legible world in which to learn about its own meaning. Being Irish and condemned to a time and place where any such meaning was deeply buried, he had to make do with his own interpretations; and so, from attempting to define himself he came to define an aspect of history through himself. The exhaustion and disillusion this caused robbed him of an innocence most people in a settled world can take for granted.

Michael O'Donovan began to discover more than just his own identity in 1916. At first the revolution distressed him because of his allegiance to boys' schools in Britain – until then his only imaginative refuge. 'And now, even if the miracle happened and Big Tim Fahy returned from Chicago with bags of money, and sent me to school in England, I should be looked on with distrust.'

Gradually, however, he came to view the Irish Rising as offering a more satisfying expression of his own personality than any he had yet come across: 'The impossible and only the impossible was law. It was, in one way, a perfect background for someone like myself who had only the impossible to hope for.'

Frank O'Connor exquisitely describes Michael O'Donovan's innocence in these years as he struggled to educate himself, to participate in the fight for freedom, while still growing towards a realisation of his own identity. But the damage which incoherence inflicts on an innocent mind is severe. There would always be for him a divorce between the real and unreal worlds, and an inability to reconcile the two. As he says: 'The imagination is a refrigerator not an incubator; it preserves the personality intact through disaster after disaster, but even when it has changed the whole world it has still changed nothing in itself, and emerges as a sort of Rip Van Winkle, older in years but not in experience.'

In the end Michael O'Donovan, as it is told in *An Only Child*, came to an intuition which contains a brilliant innocence. In the process he suffered the overthrow of his individual innocence through disappointments of the type told of in 'My Oedipus Complex', and of historical innocence through being at the mercy of an incoherent society, such as is described in *An Only Child* and 'The Duke's Children'. What he recovered was a spectrum of humane innocence, composed of a part of both he had lost – an evaluation of human beings at once private and historic: 'From the time I was a boy and could think at all, I was certain that for my own soul there was only nothingness. I knew it too well in all its commonness and weakness. But I knew that there were souls that were immortal, that even God, if He wished to, could not diminish or destroy, and perhaps it was the thought of these that turned me finally from poetry to story-telling, to the celebration of those who for me represented all I should ever know of God.'

To finish with another fable – there is a story about a troubadour whose king was captured and held for ransom at the ends of the earth. He set out to find his king, singing from countryside to countryside without success. He crossed the seas, refusing to become discouraged, discarding song after song in the attempt, abandoning his country and seeing his youth dwindle. One day, however, under the windows of an unlikely stone keep, his perseverance was rewarded; he sang three phrases of a song the king himself had written, and, coming to the window above his head, the king sang the other three.

A Sparring Partner

SHEVAWN LYNAM

Frank O'Connor literally burst in upon my life one morning in Dublin during 1942. I knew him well by sight, but I cannot recall if I had ever met him until he stood glowering down at me in my room at the Office of the United Kingdom Representative to Ireland. His voice I knew well; it was a voice one was unlikely to forget. Only a few months previously the sound of it had brought me to a standstill half-way down a corridor in the B.B.C. Then he had been delivering a moving appreciation of the British people in wartime. Now he was demanding an explanation of why British officials had ordered him to be turned back from the mail-boat on his way to England.

The situation was paradoxical, but typical. This was the O'Connor who had fought against Michael Collins in the Civil War, and then made him his hero in *The Big Fellow*. It would have been too much to expect conscientious civil servants, bent upon observing the letter of the regulations, to understand that a man who had fought against Britain and the Treaty should, in different circumstances, be one of the former enemy's most fervent supporters.

O'Connor was very far from being alone in this situation, but he was always so downright in expressing his opinions on almost any subject that it was difficult for people to forget them. He himself, on the other hand, showed no compunction about changing them radically, more often than not, I think, unconsciously. He almost seemed to delight in taking a sudden leap and, not only viewing a subject from the other end, actually embracing the opposite point of view. It helped him to keep his mind untrammelled and to avoid becoming hidebound. When he wanted to describe somebody as rather limited, he was fond of saying, 'He's one of those men who live by one simple principle.' This did not mean that he did not believe in principles, but that there were many by which to be guided.

When the war was over and we had both returned to Dublin after working for the Ministry of Information, we became neighbours for a summer in Sandymount. I was as much part of O'Connor's household as his own family and was able to watch him working at close quarters. He used to say that a writer was always writing, even when he was apparently doing nothing, and it was certainly true of him. Except for a stroll into Dublin in the afternoon, he seemed to be always at it, his most characteristic posture being in a fireside chair with a writing pad in his hand.

He was always listening for a good story and complained that during all the years he had spent among the English, for whom he had a boundless admiration, he had never once got hold of a good story, while in Ireland the supply seemed endless. He had his own selective system, and when I would come along with what I thought had the makings of something good in it, he would make me tell it orally and then classify it quite categorically as being a story or not.

His house was always full of his children's friends, and he used to protest that they made it impossible for him to work. But, in fact, he was using them all the time as a sounding board for the stories of his own childhood. They helped to keep his memories fresh. To some extent they even dictated to him. For instance, I remember an occasion when he was just about to slip a piece for the *New Yorker* into the letter-box at the General Post Office and his eight-year-old son, Miles, made some remark. 'Beastly child!' he groaned to me afterwards, with mock irritation, 'I had to bring the whole thing back and go all over the end again.'

We shared an admiration for Chekhov and discussed his

method at length. Like him, O'Connor believed that an atmosphere must emerge, being barely outlined; but people, he felt,
must be described. Like Chekhov, he felt that a moonlight night
could be brought to life simply by a dog barking and the light
shining on a piece of broken glass, whereas it made for economy
to give human beings eyes, ears, noses and mouths and, thereby,
to establish them as rapidly as possible.

I had just returned from my first journalistic assignment, and
he was as ready with help and advice as if the work were his own.
But, in the process, two things became obvious: Spain, where my
first assignment had taken me, would always divide us, and
Ireland, to which I had returned for the second time with all the
exile's enthusiasm, would always unite us. Of Spain he would
say: 'I loathe everything about that misfortunate country', over-
looking the fact that he had never been there and was singularly
ill-informed about Spanish affairs. On the other hand, when I
reminisced about the Aran islands, where I had lived for several
months, he would shudder and groan: 'God preserve me from
islands!' although I am not certain that he had ever lived in one
smaller than Ireland, which he was constantly proclaiming to be
too small by far.

Nevertheless, whatever he might say, his eyes would give him
away, and I could see that everything I ever said about Ireland
soaked in. Throughout the years it was our most constant subject
of conversation. We approached it from different backgrounds,
and although we were generally inflamed about the same aspects
of modern Ireland, my reaction was generally less violent. This
was probably due to the difference in our generations. Having
fought for the country, his was that of a disappointed lover; but
our hopes were so similar that they united us and gave us endless
matter for conjecture.

The situation I was trying to describe in my articles on Spain
was in a multitude of ways identical with that he himself had
experienced under British rule and described in *The Big Fellow*.
Yet, he refused to acknowledge any similarity and kept accusing

me of being partisan. 'For God's sake, woman,' he would say with vehemence, 'will you sit down and write about things you know something about.' At times like that he sometimes reduced me to tears.

His personality was so outsize that I was often frightened by him in those days, but I had endless proofs of his gentleness, not only in his dealings with his mother, but over small things, such as a stray dog I got attached to and which ran away, or a wounded crow I tried to save and which died in my arms in his house. He was one of the shyest people I have ever known, and when I said so to him once, he replied, 'Sure, aren't we all', adding that he would describe me more as 'fauve'. He was acutely aware of people's loneliness.

He was a daily visitor to the flat I later occupied in Fitzwilliam Square, and there he introduced me to the poetry of Emily Dickinson, to the songs of Hugo Wolf and, in a particular way, to James Joyce, whom he despised and always referred to as 'the first of the Ph.D. novelists'. *Finnegans Wake* had always been incomprehensible to me, until suddenly one evening at the house of Louis Johnston, a businessman from Belfast whose poetry he admired, O'Connor pulled down the book and started to read out loud in a broad Dublin accent; he was a superb actor. In an instant I was almost prostrate with laughter and able to understand. In many ways, however, perhaps the most important of his introductions was to Daniel Corkery's *The Hidden Ireland*, an account of life in the Big Houses when the last remnants of Gaelic society were struggling to keep going. It cropped up over and over again in our conversations in the following years.

I had just read Mary Lavin's first book of short stories, *Tales from Bective Bridge*, and was full of admiration; but O'Connor condemned it out of hand. 'That woman will never write,' he said. 'No woman can write, except, perhaps, about love. It's about the only thing they know anything about.' Yet, when I reminded him of this conversation years later, when he had become a fervent admirer of Mary Lavin's, he looked astonished and

G

disclaimed it. It was no doubt typical that what he considered to be the perfect novel, namely *Emma*, should have been written by a woman.

During the months when his home life was breaking up he said repeatedly that all he needed was two years of peace and quiet to write a novel. I knew better than to inquire what the subject would be. He was always saying that it would be impossible to write a novel about Ireland because the country had no society, but it is hard to imagine him writing about anything else. Meanwhile, the deadline for a travel book on Munster, Leinster and Connaught in a series Vesey-Fitzgerald was editing had long passed, and he asked me to undertake the research and assemble the material with him. 'You have it all in you, anyway,' he said. I never discovered whether he simply could not bring himself to the point of coping with the book, or was deliberately helping me out with a small fee at a time when I was hard put to keep going financially. I only know that he used none of the material I had so painstakingly assembled and did not tell me when the book came out. I came upon it by accident on the quays in Dublin fifteen years later.

It was during his visits to Fitzwilliam Square that I discovered his phobia about violence: I use the word phobia because he often saw violence where there was none, and sometimes refused to see it where there was plenty, as exemplified by his opposition to my anti-Franco activities and my campaigning in the Irish Association for Civil Liberties. It was a subject on which we had many clashes. When, in order to describe a young Danish writer he had just met, he said, 'Poor fellow, he's wrapped up in Hemingway, and all that violence', I knew what he was getting at; but when he would go on to put Camus and Orwell in the same class we would fight. Camus, he claimed, would never be a writer, while Orwell's *1984* was nothing but a work of appalling violence in which human beings were brought to the very edge of the precipice, something he could not bear.

After I had moved to Paris, he and his wife, Hallie, often came

through, and we always met. Then, one day I received a letter
from Hallie saying that O'Connor was coming to Paris alone and
asking me to look after him. At once I noticed a change in him.
He seemed much quieter and milder, but in the light of later
events, it may have simply been tireder. I lived on a sixth floor
without a lift, and on his constant visits he always reached the top
very puffed. He explained that he had to take the stairs easily; his
heart was not what it used to be, but there was no cause for alarm.
'Every man on a golf course in the States has a heart like mine,'
he said, 'and they live on just the same.'

I was very homesick and trying hard to get a job at home in
Ireland, and most of our talk was exile's talk. His in-laws, he
explained, were always arranging wonderful holidays for them all
in Mexico or some such place, whereas all he wanted was to go
back to Ireland where he talked of an old Georgian house he had
seen in Youghal which he would like to buy. When we visited the
ruined Cistercian abbey of Jumièges, it was the need to compare
every line with Jerpoint Abbey, Co. Kilkenny, that kept him
going around and around long after I had finished looking at it.
Pierre Emmanuel he always saw, if possible; but I doubt if there
was anybody in Paris whose company he so enjoyed as Donal
Brennan's. He was the Aer Lingus representative and knew Irish
literature in the Gaelic language exceptionally well. O'Connor
would nearly always arrive at my place quoting something
Brennan had said or humming a tune they had recalled together.

When I finally managed for the third time to give up a good
job and get home to Ireland, the O'Connors were not only there
before me, but living a hundred yards from both my new office
and my flat in the old house in Fitzwilliam Square. We met
almost daily by chance, but all too rarely by design, snatching
conversations through my office window, or during a quick
stroll along the canal banks, or for slightly longer spells during
some of the functions in Sligo in honour of Yeats. Once again,
despite the brevity of our conversations, they seemed to be always
about Ireland. It was as if we knew we were in agreement on the

basis and merely had to communicate odd details for the record as we passed by.

For instance, I had bought some books about nineteenth-century Ireland in a country hotel; he told me that I was lucky as the Americans were coming over and buying up all the books about Ireland. Or, again, I was going to Kinsale and wanted to visit the tomb of Art O'Leary on the way; he told me where to look in Kilcrea Abbey, and was in despair when I returned to say that the place was not marked and I had not found it. Or, talking of modern Irish writers, he would tell me that Jim Plunkett was the most promising and the one to watch for in the future. We shared a constant dismay at the state of Ireland's monuments, but I did not share his view of the mediaeval dinners at Bunratty Castle as vulgar. On the other hand, when the job of Curator at Yeats's Thoor Ballylee was announced and I said I felt it ought to be a prize for a poet, rather in the same way as the Oxford Chair of Poetry, he was in full agreement, but, smiling wryly, said some politician's nephew was sure to get it.

But we were no longer exiles, and often we were back on the old footing, with O'Connor attacking everything Irish and me lapping it all up. Every now and again he would find he could not stand Ireland any longer, and he and Hallie would go off to France, for which he now had the same nostalgia as he had had for Ireland when we were in Paris. On one such occasion I reminded him of an article of his I remembered having read once in the *Saturday Evening Post*, and in which he had said that the best thing about his apartment in Manhattan was the view of the boats to and from Ireland coming in and out; but he denied point-blank that he had ever said anything of the sort.

Yet, when one least expected it, his Irishness would burst out, as, for instance, in the review he wrote of Cecil Woodham-Smith's *The Great Hunger*. She was astonished and asked me to arrange for them to meet when she was in Dublin, although years earlier in Paris it was he who had said to me: 'Now that's a woman I should like to meet.' Their meeting, however, solved nothing. He continued to refuse to see that she had presented the Irish case in the manner most likely to gain it sympathy from the English reader. All that he could see was the scarcely healed wound the famine had inflicted. As a result of it, he wrote, 'the Irish people, the most musical in the world, forgot how to sing for a hundred years'. The review was a lament – a very moving one – rather than a critique, and it was paradoxical, but typical, that it should have been written in opposition to one as committed to the Irish cause and whom he admired as much as Cecil Woodham-Smith.

Apart from writing, I think that throughout his life Ireland was his deepest passion and that his criticisms belonged more to the scoldings that take place within a family than anything else. 'All men kill what they love,' he once said to me years ago in a different context, 'and I'm the worst of all at it.' True as this may have been at times in his attitude to Ireland, it was on his country and his people that he nourished his brilliant imagination. He was the most completely creative person I have known; but I felt that his creativity needed the constant contact with the world in which he had grown up. In some strange way, often when he was at his most apparently anti-Irish, I used to feel that he was grateful to me for my abiding faith in the country. It was as if I were saying for him things he would have liked to say, but felt he should not; there were too few voices in the wilderness for one of them to default.

Professor O'Connor at Stanford

WALLACE STEGNER

Frank O'Connor taught at Stanford University only two terms –
six months – but more than one former student remembers some
hour of that time as the best classroom experience of his life.
Perhaps two hundred students and auditors sat in his two-lecture
courses on the novel, another fifteen or so in his seminar in the
writing of fiction. None will forget him, for he was a great
teacher. He used to protest that he was not trained for the job,
but his humility was not persuasive to us. We knew, as he did,
with how much authority he mounted the lecture platform and
laid his books and notes on the lectern. He inhabited that raised
space more as actor than as purveyor of information.

In the grade-book and class-calendar details of teaching, including the matter of testing and judging, he was cavalier – he left
most of it to his assistants. But he was not the sort of visiting professor who, because he *is* a visitor, and untroubled by the on-
going problems of a department or a university, makes of his
appointment an opportunity for recreation and refreshment. He
carried a load, and not a light one; but he carried it in another way
than the mule-like, stubborn, one-foot-after-the-other, sanity-
and-self-saving routine that professional teachers learn. He was the
sort of high-bred horse that knows no way of taking a hill except
at a run. There is sorrow in the thought, and a rankle of guilt,
for we let him take the hills at his own chosen pace, and his service
at Stanford terminated in a slight stroke, a forerunner of the massive coronary that later killed him.

Acting is a matter that professional teachers look upon with suspicion. 'Hamming it up,' we call it, justifying our own sermons in monotone, our inert presences, our careful objectivity, our hedged judgments. But in O'Connor's classroom presence there was no ham. He was simply, always and inevitably, an interpreter, an instrument through which literature could pass and be amplified and illuminated. His sense of the audience was an actor's sense; he lacked the professional teacher's somewhat grim consciousness of how captive the student audience is, and he could not be satisfied unless he won it and held it by his own effort. Every class hour was a challenge, from his entrance to the bell; every lecture was a performance – if not always drama, at least a dramatic reading *in camera*, for he loved to read aloud.

Of course he enjoyed applause. The point is, he drove himself to earn it. Because he was not plugged into any lecture-hall circuit, because he had no accumulation of old notes and stop-gap talks, he worked like a field hand over his lectures, and he lectured four times a week. If he saw before him some apathetic face, some student sitting on his tailbone with the stunned look that said his mind was two hundred miles away on a ski slope, he groaned in spirit and cried failure. He never learned to shrug and blame a less-than-brilliant hour on post-luncheon drowsiness among the students, or the hangover from a big week-end, or youthful hormones. He blamed any such infrequent hour on himself, and suffered, and reached back into his reserves of stage experience and did something next time that would keep their eyes open and their backbones at the perpendicular.

Even he, critical of his own performance, must have had to admit that his lectures were a brilliant success. Few missed them, though attendance at class lectures is normally pretty casual; and if any did miss, their chairs were snapped up by visitors – faculty wives, random graduate students, colleagues, undergraduates from elsewhere – lurking at the doors. The window sills were commonly full of bodies, the attention was respectful, laughter went up and down the room. Moreover, they paid him the compliment of working: they stayed abreast of the reading because they did not want to miss the nuances of his interpretation and commentary. Perhaps he did not know how hard they worked for him; but I know, because my son was one of his assistants – an assistant who attended the class as religiously as if he had been taking it for credit.

A good part of that delighted response was undoubtedly response to a personality, and some of it was probably frivolous. O'Connor was a fascinating man, protean and witty. His voice was a great basso cantabile, he had a lovely brogue and eloquent eyebrows and a twinkle in his eye. He was esteemed one of the greatest short-story writers in the world (and even the way the phrase 'short stor-r-r-r-y' rolled off his tongue fluttered pulses). He had been one of the youngest, but by no means the least, of the group who made the so-called Irish Renaissance, he had acted in and directed the Abbey Theatre, had known Lady Gregory and AE and Dr Oliver St John Gogarty and could speak of Jimmy Joyce and Willie Yeats without the slightest implication of name-dropping. Willie Yeats! Marvelous.

But though this ladies'-club titillation explained some of the visitors, and was a fairly constant element in the responsiveness of students as well, no one in the room could have missed the fact that the talk about literature that came from the platform was not stale from lying in some bin, periodically sprinkled to keep it from too badly wilting. This was fresh from the garden, it had dew on it.

It was the actor in O'Connor who read aloud long passages from Trollope, or Turgenev, or Dickens, or Joyce, and simply by passing great writing through that interpreting voice of his taught his roomful more about it than they had learned from all the analyses and term papers of their previous training. But it was the artist in O'Connor who selected the passages, who commented, and who judged.

If they were mesmerized by the actor, they sometimes disputed the artist. His own creative imagination colored what he read and influenced his literary theories. Incurably synthetic, he leaped intuitively at truth; his judgments were personal, hence un-hedged, hence frequently dangerous. If every third or fourth insight was of such brilliance that it lighted up whole areas of literary experience, the other two or three might fizzle and go out in dark smoke. So some smiled at O'Connor's theory of the short story as a form dedicated to the life histories of victims, submerged populations; and they smiled again when he assured them that the length of a piece of writing had nothing to do with whether it should be called a short story or a novel: he insisted that many unlikely things, from Turgenev's *Old Portraits* to Joyce's *Ulysses*, were short stories. And thirty seconds after propounding a theory that hardly a mind in the room could accept, he would read them, with commentary, some passage of Trollope or Chekhov and send them out of the room persuaded that no one had ever waked them up in that particular way to the qualities of a particular book. He had called his study of the novel *The Mirror in the Road-way*, after Stendhal. His students swore he should write another sort of book, illustrative of the teaching of literature, and call it *Lightning in the Darkness*.

Having the freedom of a self-educated man of genius, he was not in the least method-bound. What he loved in books he had discovered for himself, and he responded with enthusiasm to any manifestation of skill, even when, as it sometimes did, it contra-dicted one of his attempts at a theory. He had a craftsman's eye for the technique that triumphantly solves a difficult problem or communicates an artistic idea with maximum effect. It is a ques-tion whether his love of skill or his abiding sense of the moral nature of literature was stronger. For though he responded to the humane and pitiful in men as in books – to Turgenev and Chekhov, say – even a writer whose temperament and moral nature repelled him, a writer such as Maupassant, could fire him with enthusiasm by the way he described a country scene, or compressed a character into a line. And though he was no ardent admirer of Joyce, he could render passages from *A Portrait of the*

Artist as a Young Man with the passion of an advocate. He did not
waste his time on academic dissection. It no more surprised him
that books contained symbols than it would have surprised him to
hear they contained words. The transmission, the meeting, the
artist's intention and the means by which it was made instantly
manifest to a reader – those were what he was after, and he
wanted them immediate, living, and whole. As a lecturer on the
novel, he was a lovely corrective to a system that too commonly
picks, dissects, damns utterly or damns with faint praise. No one
came out of Frank O'Connor's lectures a book-scorner or a book-
hater. When he opened a novel to a passage that had moved him,
they paid him the attention that Hamelin's rats paid the Pied Piper.

His writing seminar was something else, something in which
for some time he took less pleasure and from which he got far less
in the way of direct applause. Around that table he was dealing
not with literary consumers whose taste could be guided and
whose easy admiration could be stirred by the actor's performance, but with literary producers, or would-be producers,
hand-picked for talent and for nothing else. They might be narrow, egotistical, intemperate, mule-headed, self-obsessed, un-
generous, anything, so long as they had demonstrated the gift of
words. At least half of them were not students at all in the usual
sense, candidates for degrees, workers toward a liberal education.
A liberal education could go out the window tomorrow, if they
could only manage to make something of their own talent, however narrow. Brought to the university on fellowships and urged
to do nothing but write, making use of the university as much or
as little as they pleased, they probably made less use of it than they
should have, preferring instead coffee houses and the ragged little
local bohemia. It is one thing to accept a fellowship from the
Academy, another to admit that there is anything in the Academy
you might need to learn.

I don't recall everyone in that group, but I remember that it
included several who have since made literary and other sorts of
reputations. There were Larry McMurty (*The Last Picture Show*,

Leaving Cheyenne, and *Horseman, Pass By*, from the last of which was made the movie *Hud*); Peter Beagle (*The Grave's a Fine and Private Place, I See by My Outfit*); Christopher Koch, an Australian who has published a novel or two in England; James B. Hall (*Yates Paul, His Wild Flights, His Tootings*); Ken Kesey (*One Flew over the Cuckoo's Nest, Sometimes a Great Notion*); and Gurney Norman, author of some packed and delicate stories. And a few others, perhaps even some others whose names would be known. Though O'Connor had taught writing courses at Northwestern and elsewhere, he had taught no such tableful as that.

For a considerable while, at least half the time he was meeting with them, he thought he was muffling the job. Perhaps (it would not have been surprising) he half expected by precept and example to influence them in given directions, make of them writers at least partly in his own image. If he had any such idea, it quickly blew up. The insights that could set a whole lecture room to murmuring in admiration here got cold scrutiny, dissent, maybe rejection. The theories, the syntheses, were shown no quarter. His judgments and opinions were valued, apparently, no more and no less than other judgments and opinions in the seminar. They had their own stubborn convictions, some of which he strongly felt to be in error, but none of which seemed eradicable or educable. They wrote their own way, not his – their own subject-matter, their own approaches, their own language, and they did not seem to be impressed when he told them things that he had learned about the short story in forty years of hard application. He told them the short story was news, that it bent the iron, that any good story ought to be reducible to three or four lines. They thought, on the contrary, that you discovered stories the way you discovered rabbits – you went hunting for them, and they jumped out of hiding and were brought down. Some of them seemed to have a mystic belief in improvization, the impromptu; few of them valued technique as he thought it had to be valued.

They even questioned his good sense in meeting with them

twice a week. The business of a writer was to write. Why was he wasting his time in a classroom? Was he succumbing to the Academy? Was he through as a writer?

On occasion he had to think them both insolent and absurd, and they seemed to take pleasure in resisting and debating him. When class was over they followed him across the campus to the old Cellar and sat around him drinking coffee and trying to put him down. And one day Gurney Norman, feeling the oncoming spring's effects on his spirits, put on in the seminar room a recording of 'My First Confession', so that when O'Connor entered the room he heard O'Connor reading O'Connor. He thought he was being ridiculed. Why would anyone do a thing like that unless to intimate that the teacher was in love with the sound of his own voice?

He thought he had lost the class – had never had it. He thought there was such a gap between them that they would submit to learning nothing from him. Their casual obscenity troubled him too – that revolution had gone further than he could approve. Hoping to teach them some temperance of language, he told them he couldn't read their stuff aloud in that mixed class. If they felt they had to write that way, they would have to read their own. They did, with relish, and not the least of their relish was the embarrassment they caused him. By the end of the winter term he was ready to admit defeat; he hated the thought of another quarter of it.

But when he returned after a week of vacation he found them almost suspiciously friendly. They seemed glad to see him. They acted as if they had chafed under the enforced suspension of the class. Gurney Norman came to him full of contrition at the mis-understood joke; far from being critical of O'Connor, he wor-shipped him. It dawned on O'Connor that when they followed him across the campus to the Cellar (he thought of them as a bunch of dogs pursuing a wounded fox, they thought of them-selves as a bunch of puppies) they followed him because they couldn't bear to let the session end after the scheduled two hours.

Far from scorning the sessions, they did their best to make them four hours long.

And that was something more than the triumph of an actor before an essentially inert audience. In the writing seminar the actor had no place and the teacher was only another writer. The class was not an audience and the response was not applause, but argument, discussion, debate, dissension, assertion and denial, each one defending his territory and trying to drive off intruders and aggressors who threatened his theory, his art or his ego. Not one of them had the slightest doubt that their sessions were exhilarating and useful. Not one of them would have admitted writing, or wanting to write, like Frank O'Connor. Not one of them could have or would have denied him his right to be power-fully and excitingly himself. The actor, used to practising his public art before an audience of consumers, had simply misread their response. The artist eventually understood it for what it was, their acceptance of him as catalyst, provocateur, fellow artist and even, in ways they would hardly have admitted, master.

How much he actually changed their writing, their convictions or their language is a question. Not much, probably. But he made them prove themselves against standards that, whether they agreed with them or not, they had to confront and consider. He offered them no permissive or submissive chairman for their debates. When they assaulted him with their barbaric yawp, he told them what it was. He gave them an example of what human-ity, cultivation, learning and sensitivity could come to in a fully matured writer, and he made them respect the combination even when they wouldn't imitate it.

And one final thing. As with those standard authors whom he could not fully agree with or respect, but whose skill so often inspired his entirely ungrudging admiration, he responded with robust enthusiasm to these young writers when they wrote well, even if he disapproved of everything their writing seemed to aim at. He could not resist good writing, and he knew it when he read it, however much it might offend his sense of the moral obligation of literature and however much he might doubt the total humanity of the writer. The seminar that at first troubled him with a sense of his own inadequacy was finally his enthusiasm and delight. And theirs. It was a continuation of that seminar, not a lecture course full of appreciative consumers, that he was coming back to Stanford to teach. Death cut him off, and the seminar he was booked for will never know what it missed. But those who sat in the seminar of 1961 can tell them.

Little Monasteries

BRENDAN KENNELLY

Frank O'Connor's fame as a writer of short stories has somewhat
overshadowed his achievement as a poet. It was as a poet, in fact,
that he began his writing career, and he produced a number of
original poems. Then he turned to the short story form and
dedicated the greater part of his energy to that. But once a poet,
always a poet, practising or otherwise, and while O'Connor
created several masterpieces in his chosen form, he also continued his service to poetry, mainly by way of translation. His
King, Lords, & Commons is a monumental work, containing
excellent poems, the most impressive of which seems to me to be
the translation of Brian Merryman's long poem, 'The Midnight
Court', vibrant with a kind of visionary bawdiness and up-
roarious spiritual gusto, perfectly capturing the curious mixture
of verbal licence and emotional inhibition, of audacity and frustration, that Merryman discovered in eighteenth-century Gaelic
Ireland. O'Connor's uncanny insight into the poetry of that time
and that society enabled him to bring a remote eighteenth-
century poet right into the heart of our times, portraying both the
frustration and the ebullience with a vitality of language that
Merryman himself would have loved. Here, for example, is one of
these sexually frustrated young women,

> *Heartsick, bitter, dour and wan,*
> *Unable to sleep for want of a man.*

compelled to lie in a lukewarm bed, desperately revealing her vain stratagems to get a man. It is frantic, funny and sad.

> *Every night when I went to bed*
> *I'd a stocking of apples beneath my head;*
> *I fasted three canonical hours*
> *To try and come round the heavenly powers;*
> *I washed my shift where the stream ran deep*
> *To hear my lover's voice in sleep;*
> *Often I swept the woodstack bare,*
> *Burned bits of my frock, my nails, my hair,*
> *Up the chimney stuck the flail,*
> *Slept with a spade without avail;*
> *Hid my wool in the lime-kiln late*
> *And my distaff behind the churchyard gate; ...*
> *But 'twas all no good and I'm broken-hearted*
> *For here I'm back at the place I started;*
> *And this is the cause of all my tears*
> *I am fast in the rope of the rushing years,*
> *With age and need in lessening span,*
> *And death beyond, and no hopes of a man.*

From beginning to end the poem bristles with this sort of vitality, giving the urbane couplet which Merryman took from contemporary English poetry a shock of earthy realism. *Kings, Lords, & Commons* is full of such treasures; it is fair to say that in many cases O'Connor created completely new poems, as Ezra Pound does in his translations from the Chinese. In 1963 O'Connor produced his last book of poems, *The Little Monasteries*. It contains twenty poems, all of which may be looked on as new creations, obviously the work of a dedicated poet and a scrupulous craftsman. This small collection of poems contains some of Frank O'Connor's finest work.

The book falls neatly into three thematic divisions. It is concerned with nature, poets and love. The forms are in many cases simple but effective, the rhythms frequently predictable but always strong, the idiom an impressive blend of a modern conversational tone and a unique kind of passionate formality.

Above all the poems are intensely dramatic in mood, tone and structure. O'Connor came more and more to believe in the concentrated urgency and intensity of the dramatic lyric. When he read poetry aloud, he made it a dramatic experience, scorning the sophisticated timidity and urbane spinelessness of so many contemporary poetry-readers. He shamelessly and delightedly wrung the last shred of drama from every poem he read, and, in most cases, he communicated both the drama and the delight to his audience. In *The Little Monasteries* we shall see how effectively he explores and develops the dramatic lyric.

Only the first two poems deal directly with nature. 'The Seasons' is exquisitely wrought, rich in vowel music, and immediately striking for its precision and fullness of detail. It opens with a description of Autumn, marvellously portraying the curious mixture of fatigue and superfluity characteristic of that season. Every line is concrete and evocative, making a conscious but judicious use of alliteration; notice how the word 'fall', used both as noun and verb, opens and closes the stanza, so that what we get is a bursting picture of ripe fullness enclosed in a framework of finality. The unmistakable feeling of Autumn fills those lines.

> *Fall is no man's travelling time;*
> *Tasks are heavy; husbandmen*
> *Heed the low light, lingering less.*
> *Lightly their young drop from the deer,*
> *Dandled in the faded fern;*
> *Fiercely the stag stalks from the hill,*
> *Hearing the herd in clamorous call;*
> *Cobbled the mast in windless woods,*
> *Weary the corn upon its canes,*
> *Colouring the brown earth.*
> *Endless the thorns that foul the fence*
> *Which frames the hollow of some house;*
> *The hard dry ground is filled with fruit,*
> *And by the fort, hard from their height,*
>   *Hazelnuts break and fall.*

H

The other three seasons are described with the same delicacy and detail. 'The Seasons' is purely objective in its appreciation of nature. 'In the Country' is similarly appreciative, but the poet intrudes to tell us that though he is willing to praise the singing birds, he is also happy about his own capacity for expression. The result of this sense of excellence within and outside himself is to make him ask the source of all excellence not to be too hard on him when the hour for judging poets is at hand, suggesting, perhaps, that the final fruit of any human perfection is the realisation of its ultimate inadequacy.

> *A hedge of trees is all around;*
>   *The blackbird's praise I shall not hide;*
> *Above my book so smoothly lined*
>   *The birds are singing far and wide.*

> *In a green cloak of bushy boughs*
>   *The cuckoo pipes his melodies –*
> *Be good to me, God, on Judgment Day! –*
>   *How well I write beneath the trees!*

In the second section there are several poems dealing with various kinds of poets. It begins with a four-line poem in which an old poet prays and gives thanks to God for continued inspiration.

> *God be praised who ne'er forgets me*
>   *In my art so high and cold*
> *And still sheds upon my verses*
>   *All the magic of red gold.*

Nobody knew better than O'Connor with what intensity poets were feared and loved in ancient Ireland, and, in 'The Thirsty Poet', he records a poet's gratitude to a king's daughter because she slaked his thirst. This is the diametrical opposite of James Stephens's poem in which he denounces a 'whey-faced slut' of a woman for refusing him a drink. Stephens satirises meanness; O'Connor celebrates generosity:

> Blessings on King Donal's daughter,
>   Gracious Ethna, good indeed,
> Who, when I had cased the township
>   For rat poison,
> Sent me two and thirty wry-necked
>   Harnessed hauliers'
>   Load of mead.

'The Angry Poet', on the contrary, displays a vicious spirit; the poet is here in a bitter rage and he condemns the targets of his anger – the hound, the lackey, the master and his wife – to a lifetime of foul intimacy. It is in 'The Ex-Poet', however, that the real O'Connor emerges. He is here dealing with one of these lonely voices, those solitary people that fill his short stories. The ex-poet is such a figure, a drab spiritual pariah on the fringe of society, moving anonymously towards a casual oblivion. This is an area where O'Connor's compassionate imagination is most penetrating and active, and, with terrifying bareness, he presents the fate of the lonely outcast.

> No woman now shall be his mate,
> No son nor daughter share his fate,
> No thigh beside his thigh repose –
> Solitary the ex-poet goes.

It is in the third section of the book, the love-poetry, that O'Connor is at his best. The range of these poems is far wider, the theme is obsessively explored from various angles and, above all, their essentially *dramatic* character is always compelling. In all the poems, except one, 'The Nun of Beare', it is the man or the ghost of the man who speaks, usually dramatising his loss. The poems range from the facetious to the profound, from the realistic to the supernatural. O'Connor is true to all tones, discovering an appropriate idiom and form for the prevailing mood.

In *The Little Monasteries*, O'Connor produces some love-poems which must surely be among the best in Irish literature. There is no trace of embarrassment, no sense of unbearable intimacy, no sentimental overstatement, or romantic distortion of the reality. He saves it by irony, passion and sometimes even a spirit of mischief as in, for example, 'Advice to Lovers', where the counsel is one of jovial indifference, which gives the lover who possesses it a gay resilience to practically everything. The cheeky metre is in tune both with the gumption of the man who offers the advice and the audacity of the lover who would accept it.

> *The way to get on with a girl*
> *Is to drift like a man in a mist,*
> *Happy enough to be caught,*
> *Happy to be dismissed.*
>
> *Glad to be out of her way,*
> *Glad to rejoin her in bed,*
> *Equally grieved or gay*
> *To learn that she's living or dead.*

The supernatural element enters in 'The Dead Lover', in which O'Connor compresses a fifty-verse ninth-century poem into nineteen austerely hewn stanzas. It tells how Fohad, leader of a band of mercenaries, elopes with the wife of another mercenary chief. He is killed in battle, but returns to keep his tryst. This is one of the most dramatic of all the poems. Fohad's ghost addresses the girl with shattering directness.

> *Silence, girl! What can you say?*
> *My thoughts are not of you, they stray;*
> *I think of nothing else tonight*
> *Except the battlefield and fight.*
>
> *My headless body tossed aside*
> *Lies on the slope whereon I died,*
> *And in that heap my head you see*
> *Near those of men who died with me.*

A lovers' tryst is waste of breath
Beside the final tryst with death,
And so the lovers' tryst we made
I can keep only as a shade.

With dramatic simplicity O'Connor portrays the lover's ghost looking back on his own dead body, thinking of the fight and of his love.

I am not the first in body's heat
Who found some outland woman sweet,
And though our parting tryst be drear
It was your love that brought me here.

It was for love alone I came,
Leaving my gentle wife in shame:
Had I but known what would befall
How gladly would I have shunned it all.

He confesses his love for her, at the same time pointing out how futile is her love for him.

Why should you spend a night of dread
Alone among the unburied dead?

He must part with her because the dawn, which severs mortal from immortal, is near. The sundering is complete.

From human things I must take flight
After my men with the first light;
Already the night's end has come;
Do not stay here, back to your home!

He tells her to raise a 'great tomb' above him that he may be remembered and praised, and the poem closes with a heartbreaking statement about lonely descent into the grave.

Now my pierced body must descend
To torture where the fiends attend;
Worldly love is a foolish thing
Beside the worship of Heaven's king.

It is the blackbird! Once again
He calls at dawn to living men;
My voice, my face are of the dead.
Silence! What is there to be said?

There is a deft partial reversal in 'On the Death of His Wife' in which the living man mourns the dead woman. We are plunged at the beginning into a mood of desolation and loss which is sustained throughout.

I parted from my life last night,
A woman's body sunk in clay:
The tender bosom that I loved
Wrapped in a sheet they took away.

The dark mood of lamentation in this poem is continually offset by other poems of a much lighter tone, wavering between seriousness and flippancy. And so in 'Women' we meet a lover who appears to be wryly amused by his own lack of prejudice towards women.

No fanaticism I share
For blue or black in someone's eye
Or the colour of her hair.

In fact, the only criticism one can make of this man is that he has no criticism to make of women; his fault is that he sees no fault.

And all may hear what I would say –
In women, such is my disgrace,
I never found a thing astray.

The point of the poem, however, is not that he is indiscriminate through ignorance, but that he is tolerant through knowledge. As he neatly and rather glibly lists for us those qualities which he insists he does not require in women, we realise that he is deeply aware of feminine merits and defects. In stating his acceptance of the many limitations of women, he reveals himself as an acute

observer of their attractions. The uncritical liberal is in fact a
scrupulous connoisseur.

> *I don't require them cold or warm;*
>   *Widows have knowledge and good sense*
> *But there is still a certain charm*
>   *In a young girl's inexperience.*
>
> *I like them in church, demure and slow,*
>   *Solemn without, relaxed at home;*
> *I like them full of push and go*
>   *When love has left me overcome.*
>
> *I find no fault in them, by God,*
>   *But being old and gone to waste*
> *Who still are girls at forty odd –*
>   *And every man may suit his taste.*

It is difficult to realise with what industry and tenacity O'Connor worked at these poems. His finest love-poem, 'The Nun of
Beare', was written and re-written over a period of at least thirty
years. It first appeared in *The Oxford Book of Modern Verse*, edited
by Yeats, in 1936, and the finished version is in *The Little Monasteries* (1963). What strikes one most of all about the changes in
the poem over the years is the way in which O'Connor insisted on
dramatising it more and more. In the *Oxford Book*, it is a straight-
forward lyric; in *The Little Monasteries*, it is a dramatic poem with
voices. O'Connor had for many years accepted the view of the
editors of the original Old Irish poem, Kuno Meyer and Gerard
Murphy, but as time passed, he became convinced that:

it is really a series of lyrics from a lost eighth century romance
which was edited in the tenth or eleventh century to give it a
fictitious homogeneity, and that this rehandling is largely responsible for its formless appearance ...

The heroine of the romance would seem to have been originally
the Goddess of Munster, though the story teller did not know this.
All he knew was the tradition of the various marriages she had
celebrated with the Munster Kings, and he regarded her as an Irish

Mary Magdalen. This is how she appears in the first lyric. Then Saint Cummine, 'whose knowledge of the byways of sexual behaviour is entitled to rank beside Kinsey's', in the words of one Irish scholar, is brought to deal with her. It is clear that at the crisis of the story, The Nun challenged Christ to spend the night with her, and after He appeared, was converted and reconciled to the idea of old age. (*Kilkenny Magazine*, Spring 1962)

The dominating voices in the final version of the poem are the Nun and Cummine. The poem is charged with the pathos filling the memories of this archetypal lover who sadly contrasts the excitement of her youth with her present uneventful life as an ageing spiritual recluse.

> *I, the old woman of Beare,*
> *Who wore dresses ever-new*
> *Have so lost the shape I wore*
> *Even an old one will not do.*
>
> *And my hands as you can see*
> *Are but bony wasted things,*
> *Hands that once would grasp the hand*
> *Clasp the royal neck of kings.*

Cummine's interjections are relatively quiet, and towards the end the old woman has moments when she harrowingly realises the truth of her position.

> *Floodtide!*
> *And the ebb with hurrying fall;*
> *I have seen many, ebb and flow,*
> *Ay, and now I know them all.*

In complete contrast to the old woman of Beare is Eve, in the poem of that name. Whereas the old woman yearns for youthful excitement, Eve is full of remorse for her mistake in Eden. The two poems present a dramatic contrast between the old woman's indomitable lust for life, and the original mother of men yelping about the consequences of her sin. Of the two, the old woman of Beare is by far the more admirable. Despite her consciousness of lost beauty and her sense of being ravaged by time, she is remark-able for a serene note of reconciliation in her thoughts, for her spirit of goodwill towards her many lovers, and for the sad last remnants of desire. Whereas, in the case of Eve, it is easy enough to see not only how she became the first unfortunate mother of humanity, but also how she must have been the world's first nagging wife.

> *Dreadful was the choice I made,*
> *I who was once a mighty queen;*
> *Dreadful, too, the price I paid –*
> *Woe, my hand is still unclean!*

> *I plucked the apple from the spray,*
> *Because of greed I could not rule;*
> *Even until their final day*
> *Women still will play the fool.*

> *Ice would not be anywhere,*
> *Wild white winter would not be;*
> *There would be no hell, no fear*
> *And no sorrow but for me.*

I have tried to give some idea of the variety and vitality of this poetry which O'Connor rescued and translated from distant centuries. With the exception of four, all the poems in *The Little Monasteries* come from the period between the seventh and the twelfth centuries. O'Connor was that rare, happy combination – a brilliant creative writer and a scrupulous scholar. In *King, Lords, & Commons* and *The Little Monasteries*, O'Connor has given us a body of poems which brilliantly re-create personalities and situations of an ancient world and, more important still, help to order and illuminate the world in which we live.

Reminiscences from France

DONAL BRENNAN

Even in the sultry heat of late summer, when Parisians relinquish their city to tourists, guides and waiters, the arches of the Rue de Castiglione lend a shade and coolness to the offices which they shelter. It was in the Rue de Castiglione in the sultry heat of such a late summer, with a thunderstorm pending, that I first met Frank O'Connor, when he walked out of the heat into my office to read the Irish papers and to make some banal travel arrangements. He continued to call during all his subsequent visits to France, and they were many.

France was a country which he loved deeply and was irritated by in equal measure. With his nostalgia for the possibilities of development which a truly Gaelic–Norman fusion of cultures could have represented for Ireland if it had not been totally disrupted and deformed by wars, repressions and imposed alien institutions, he saw in France, its architecture, literature and total cultural self-confidence, the full flower and impressive reality of what might have been in Ireland.

Frank was a neat and even picturesque dresser, who, as an artist, was fully conscious of his impressive appearance: the great brow, the nobly formed head, the musical voice; similarly, his handwriting, distinctive, legible, neat, portrayed the attentive and meticulous writer; but in mundane practical matters of money or of transport, of time-tables, of schedules or of documentation he was less than gifted – in fact, he was a child. He was, however, a very clever child, who gave a beaming smile to the nearest victim available and then threw the whole problem into his hands while he went on to discuss more serious things like history or literature or the asinine behaviour of his latest pet aversion. ('Good heavens, man! There is no spark at all there! The man's a fool! I'm surprised you can't see that!')

However, on that hot day in the late summer of 1956 when he had flung his transport problems in Paris on to my desk we lunched in the 'Belle Aurore' on the Marché Saint-Honoré, and for two hours he treated me, a comparative stranger, to a display of his deep knowledge, and love, of French literature, which impressed me very much then and remained always in my mind. More pleasing still was his manner of drawing on Gaelic and English sources for comparisons, and he was the first to point out to me how close many French proverbs are to Irish ones. Furthermore, he had one of the finer attributes of human nature, he was a good listener, but if he heard anything which he might utilise he would note it down carefully and shamelessly before you, so that one could sometimes feel indeed that 'a chiel's amang us takin' notes and faith, he'll print it'. And so Frank would if it was worth printing.

He had the gift of seizing the adumbration of a quarter-idea, twisting it, changing it, until suddenly, by some strange transmutation, it had become something vivid and genuine so that one would momentarily flatter oneself that the idea was indeed one's own.

That day in the 'Belle Aurore' I remember vividly how he pointed out that the French and Irish were a match for one another in literary satire and bitterness, and he quoted Aodhgan O'Raithille and Leconte de Lisle with equal impressiveness. I can still hear the rich Cork accents, with the wonderful resonance, as he quoted, while the people at adjacent tables eavesdropped:

> *Vous vivez lâchement sans rêve, sans dessein,*
> *Plus vieux, plus décrépits que la terre inféconde*
> *Châtrés dès le berceau par le siècle assassin*
> *De toute passion, vigoureuse et profonde!*

(As cowards you live, without a dream or plan,
More old, more decrepit, than your infertile earth
From all profound and virile passions of man
By our assassin era, castrated at birth!)

'There, man, there's great stuff! Sure any Irish poet might say that about Ballyex today!' and he mentioned an Irish town which appeared to hold disagreeable memories for him.

The visits to France were numerous, and it is against this French background that I see him most vividly, eating in 'Le Volney', discoursing for hours in a flat on the Île Saint-Louis – on a balcony with a majestic view up and down the Seine; drinking lightly in a famous bistro on the Rue Daunou; and always people listened with pleasure because he never bored and he brought out the best in others. Because, whatever about his origins, O'Connor was undoubtedly one of Nature's patricians. He was an artist and a good one and he knew it and made no secret of that knowledge. In other things he was mistrusting of himself and his personality and could at times betray what to me seemed an amazing lack of self-confidence. But he was always the patrician, with a keen distaste for oppression, violence, meanness, flatulent or vulgar conversation. He could enjoy a French story which might be 'grivois' but humorous; he would not tolerate the teller of salacious stories.

He had his loyalties too. It was in Harry's bar in the Rue Daunou before a British election. We were talking and drinking quietly and behind us was an English party of whom three were journalists – one rather well-known. The latter made some vivid and disparaging comments on Mr Anthony Eden and Mr Harold Macmillan. Finally his comments hovered close to the edge of vulgarity. O'Connor turned to the speaker, who was sitting right beside him, and said: 'I don't know Eden, but I have met Macmillan and I as an Irishman can tell you that he is very courteous, highly intelligent and highly astute.' The Englishman in a French bar dropped back into his more polite self and did not resent the implied rebuke.

One night on the Île Saint-Louis an American lady asked him what he considered his most perfect translation from the Gaelic.

He swung around to me, the great eyebrows lifted. 'And what do you think?'

I instanced diffidently:

> *Fagaim le h'uadhact e go n-eirigeann mo croidhe se*
> *Mar eirigeas an gaoi no mar scaipeas an seo*

from Raftery, and added his own:

> *I give you my word that the heart in me rises*
> *As when the wind rises and all the mists go.*

'Now do you hear the Connaughtman talking?' he said sardonically, but he continued the quotation and then went on to 'Valentine Brown' while the room was quiet there above the Seine as he declaimed.

He really knew French literature and its by-ways. Once when someone mentioned Alain-Fournier's *Le Grand Meaulnes* as an effort by a very young man at what Joyce had achieved in *Stephen Hero*, he said: 'Heavens, man, you shouldn't make that comparison', but went on to ask us if we had read the *Letters* of Alain-Fournier, which very few professional students of French literature have read. His reading range of French literature was extraordinarily wide, and stretched from Montaigne to Sartre, and strolled down many by-ways on the literary road. He greatly admired Montherlant.

Again it is an evening in the Rue Daunou. A French professor advances the argument that the Wexford rebellion of 1798 was a purely religious rebellion like the Vendée and in no way related to the secular or Protestant rebellion of the United Irishmen in the North based on French Revolutionary ideas. O'Connor is genuinely hurt. 'Good God, man, you don't know what you are saying!' and he gives a lecture, indeed a vivid word picture of the

spread of the French idea in Ireland, finishing with his own translation of Sliabh na mBan:

> Blithe as a blackbird on a green bough singing
> Would be my heart if the French would come
> If I could see them in the morning early
> On a sunny upland by Sliabh na mBan

then he puts back his head and sings: "'Twas early early in the
Spring' in a moving voice. All enjoyed it and there were hard-
boiled French and English journalists in the audience.

Frank O'Connor could be argumentative and disputatious,
almost maddeningly so at times, but there was only one subject on
which he became flamingly and passionately angry; that was the
Great Famine of 1846–7 and for the criminal folly and haphazard
palliative measures adopted by the authorities at that time he had
only one word: genocide. For this reason Cecil Woodham-
Smith's book angered him, and he said so, loudly. He was pleased
when I sent him a long review of the book from Professor
Frechet of Lille University, which agreed broadly with his own
opinions, which saw the results of the Famine prolonged to today
and saw them particularly extending to the Parnell period in
which he was so deeply interested.

For this reason he had great admiration for Wilfred Scawen
Blunt – 'an Englishman with a completely free soul' as he called
him – and he would quote a verse from Blunt's 'Canon of
Aughrim' about the evicted peasants of the West in a moving
fashion:

> Deep in the gulf of your cities they lie, the poor lorn creatures,
> Made in God's image once, His folded innocent sheep,
> Now misused and profaned, in speech and form and features
> Living like devils and dying like dogs in incestuous sleep.

But he was fully aware of the noble and cultured civilisation of
England which had bred Blunt, and he drew my attention with
deep admiration to a passage which he called 'poetry in casual

correspondence'. Blunt was describing Wilton, the family seat of the Herberts:

> Wilton is the paradise of England with its three rivers eternally beautiful and unchanged while its owners change and perish. One passes by and find Herberts living there, happily idling their lives away as one finds swallows year after year nesting in a village, and one imagines them to be the same Herberts, as one imagines the other to be the same swallows.

And he pointed out that Kuno Meyer's translation of the eighth-century Irish poem 'That Rath on the Hill' had a similar idea more neatly put.

He was pleased, too, that the Commissaire of Police at Le Bourget Airport had read his short stories and his harmless vanity was obviously flattered when the Commissaire called him 'Maître' and personally escorted him and his wife through the state controls at the airport. Such a typical French touch from the representative of a nation which still treats its writers with the respect and admiration given by other nations to film-stars, pop-singers or tycoons gave O'Connor genuine pleasure. 'God, Don, maybe the local sergeant at home will salute a poor writer someday', and he guffawed with laughter at the thought. 'Imagine Brendan [Behan] or Paddy Kavanagh getting a salute in Baggot Street!' and he laughed again on the steps of the aircraft.

I genuinely pleased him once in Desirrier's restaurant in the Place Péreire. He had quoted the 'old Man's' – 'How could we dream that he could comb grey hair', and I said that Yeats had lifted it from Mac an Bhaird through Clarence Mangan: 'That's a remarkable statement, a truly remarkable statement,' he said. I instanced:

> Theirs were not souls wherein dull time could domicile decay or house decrepitude.

He looked up and signalled the waiter urgently: 'Garçon, garçon! S'il vous plaît.' The waiter came and O'Connor asked for the best bottle of Burgundy in the house. I shudder to think of what it cost him. But he beamed. 'The two quotations were in my head all these years and dammit, Don, I never put them together, after Ronsard; after Mangan!' and he beamed again as if he were teasing the long-dead Yeats.

So it was that I met him and knew him best for many years in Paris, and I think always of the patrician, the unrecognised French-language expert, the despiser of Carleton (and how we disagreed on that!), the hater of fake or piosity, of snuffling smugness, of the uncultured philistines who so often control purse-strings in the modern world ('God, man, when you face some of the people I face, it's G-R-E-A-T-T to love old stones'), the kind and dignified scholar who walked at his ease with professors of the Sorbonne.

He died suddenly and one found that 'le monde avait rétréci un peu' as they say in a land he loved well.

The Platonist

MAURICE SHEEHY

Michael, in so far as I can think objectively about him, had
enormous courage – a courage based on integrity and a frighten-
ingly honest self-appraisal. He disclaimed physical bravery himself – although I know of no instance of his lack of it – but it
seemed almost as if his intellectual fallibility were getting in the
way of his moral and intellectual courage. Only those who retain
a very pure innocence can afford to reveal themselves to others –
and to shatter human convention with abandon. Michael had that
innocence, and its daughter, simple courage. It was that innocence
which enabled one to discuss any aspect of human integrity with
him in complete confidence. It is not that one expected him to be
always right in his views in an objective sense, but he took for
granted that you would be utterly committed to the implications
of your principles in a subjective sense. On less important subjects,
opinions, academic views, methods and applications he could be
dogmatic, changeable, emotional and even slightly hysterical at
times. But the two kinds of subject-matter were not unconnected:
on any subject he was intolerant of intellectual dishonesty or
moral cowardice.

Michael himself professed to have little time for abstractions or
abstract theories, although he called himself a rationalist once. The
prejudice came from an abuse which plagued him in the Ireland of
his youth and early manhood. For him the habit of thinking in
purely abstract and woolly notions about highly emotional
matters like nationalism, patriotism and religion had got out of

hand, and often led to an appalling manipulation of public opinion and a dulling of the sensitivities necessary for real personal commitment and sincerity. Formally he knew little about philosophy, and his own use of philosophical terms and his opinions about philosophers are frequently untrustworthy. Yet Michael was more of a philosopher than most and he would have had less caustic asides for the philosophers had he had a first-hand experience of its disciplines. The essence of his own special medium, for example, the short story, was that it be the expression of a universal experience. Not an individual experience, he would point out to his students, but an individual expression of a universal experience. Had he realised that by 'abstraction' the philosophers mean no more than the ordinary mental function of 'abstracting' the universally applicable from individual experience, he might easily have been diverted to epistemology.

He would have been shocked, and then amused, had he known how some of his ideas resembled the Aristotelian–Thomist theory of knowledge. He spoke of the mind taking on the forms of the objects it knows, and of the subject of perception becoming the object perceived and likened this process of 'object becoming the subject' to the thing photographed photographing the camera. This was a notion he carried much farther. 'Bethlehem itself was merely an interesting object which the Roman Empire had studied with amusement till suddenly it opened its eyes and the Roman Empire was no more.' Questioned about the form in his own writings, he replied: 'It's not imposed form, but the form of life itself. I want form to follow a man's life or a man's character. The form is inherent in the experience. Chekhov is wonderful for that: the completely organic form. I think fundamentally it goes back to a man's attitude to life. In Chekhov you feel that life is dictating to him; in Joyce he is dictating to life. I'm not saying for an instant that the writer is passive to life. He is *giving* himself to it. He just says to life, "Oh, *that's* what you mean? That's grand! Carry on!"'

Michael's philosophy was worked out hand in hand in his

writings and in his personal life. His honesty and his courage would not have it otherwise. However we read his life, the key to understanding it is to be found in what he wrote. Behaviour and thought were for him the same. He did not hesitate once to write to a pillar of religion over what he saw was a sordid action and say that 'it was useless for them to think of themselves as Christians until they stopped behaving as savages'. Later he commented in a letter 'these people with their Thomas Aquinas do not know the most rudimentary thing about civilised life'. But this was a rejection of hypocrisy not Aquinas, as we see in his views on the natural law. To a friend he wrote: 'there are occasions when we all feel guilt and remorse; we all want to turn back time. But even if we were able, things would go in precisely the same way, because the mistakes we make are not in our judgments but in our natures. It is only when we do violence to our natures that we are justified in our regrets, and neither of us is capable of that. We are what we are, and within our limitations we have made our own efforts. They seem puny in the light of eternity, but they didn't at the time, and they weren't.'

The struggle is essentially in man himself. 'We do not change people through the things in them that we would wish to change, but through the things that they themselves wish to change.' The highest ideals can be destroyed through lack of integrity and decency. 'What a noble thing it is to revive a language, and what a mean thing it becomes when it falls into the hands of louts!' was his comment on certain efforts to revive Irish.

Inevitably, it was a turbulent journey for him from the beginning. From his earliest days he had a vision, largely nurtured by his mother, of far-off Truth and Love and Beauty, and he spent his life trying to realise it. For years he sought this goal in the beauty and perfection of human endeavour, impatiently resisting the hint that its realisation might be beyond human ability. Yet he knew that the use of human talent had something vital to do with it, and he aimed at perfection in his own endeavours. 'Responsibilities are things one owes to oneself, not to others,' he wrote. But, for all his courage, he was sensitive and vulnerable, and the honesty of his mind was challenged by sham and deceit which often accompanied apparent claims for truth. Of a friend he was heard to say: 'One of the things I like about him is that he doesn't argue to win.' His exaggerated sense of honesty made him hesitate to search for truth in loveless and aridly conventional surroundings. 'Life', he wrote, 'cannot get better until people themselves get better, and people cannot begin to get better until they have set themselves free of the devil's snare of ignorance and prejudice and stop talking of capitalists, Freemasons, Jesuits and Yids.' Sensitive, as all innocent lovers are, he lashed out, violently at times, at the insensitive mass of ignorance and mediocrity. Little minds became frightened. The complacent and the righteous, offended, closed ranks against this apparent Savonarola.

He made mistakes and left himself open to the enthusiastic condemnation of his relieved opponents. The odds seemed all against him, yet the vision nurtured in the days of childish innocence supported him. He had experienced truth and love and beauty in tender maternal care – and thereafter knew for certain that Love was honest and gentle and beautiful. Yet in a way that first experience robbed him of his freedom. Of his mother's death he wrote: 'Then only did I realize that the horror that had haunted me from the time I was a child . . . had happened at last . . . and . . . it made no difference to me that I was fifty and a father myself.' But the event was a mixed tragedy. The dimension of his journey had irrevocably altered. Now he was free to find his own mould for the tempestuous course. Like Abelard he met Heloise in class and through her love a new light was thrown on his early dream. It seemed that love and truth are no less real, however entangled in man-made trappings. Generous human love suggested Love Itself. He re-set his sights on a dim hope. But how could any man accept the vast implications of this hope? 'The eternal silence of those infinite spaces terrifies me', he wrote, echoing Pascal. Why should he – who knew more than most of love – be cherished by Love? 'As though any reasonable man

could be vain enough to believe himself worthy of immortality.'
And yet the peace that came with human love seemed to suggest
that however unworthy in himself, man was made for this very
thing.

Impatient always with the 'philosophers who know it all' – the
single volume by a philosopher in his fine library was the *Enneads*
of Plotinus – he bent his own talent to seek the meaning of his recaptured hope. Like Mozart 'before he passed through the horror
of death's night' Michael too 'set himself to sound the middle C
of faith'. He started off with a thought which, unknown to him,
is a fundamental concept with every philosopher. 'Truth is
subjective and objective and there is no greater truth than this.'
Of objective truth we can know only our own ignorance. He was
a Platonist at heart, and the vision of the One was too immense
for its creature. 'From the time I was a boy and could think at all,
I was certain that for my own soul there was only nothingness.'
Not because a soul couldn't be immortal, but because 'I knew it
too well in all its commonness and weakness.'

Ironically perhaps, the other Irish writer who springs to mind
was a philosopher – the only one of consequence ever born on the
island. Eriugena was a Platonist, and he too was appalled at the
immensity of God, and believed that to understand our ignorance
of God was the height of human knowledge. On this fundamental
fact he built his philosophy.

Both these writers have been widely misunderstood, and
Michael, like Eriugena, has been wrongly judged by lesser
men. To assert, as these two did, that authority proceeds from
right reason and never reason from authority, was frightening to
weaker minds. And despite frequent accusations to the contrary
there is not the slightest trace of the philosophical freethinker or
rationalist about either. What Michael wrote about Chekhov (the
writer he admired perhaps above all others) he was also saying
about himself: 'He always writes as a moralist, but his morality
is no longer the morality of the group, it is the short-story writer's
morality of the lonely individual soul.' In the final analysis the

honest man is on his own. 'Whether we are good or bad, we are still lonely, but all the same it is better to be lonely and good.' Michael admired John XXIII and John Kennedy enormously: the Pope who restored dignity to the individual and liberated him from the death of mere conformity to convention and the President who proclaimed excellence in the individual soul as an aim in itself. His moral sense was apprehensive that we might all become 'coffin-makers, all makers of categories, all refusing to love our neighbour or fish in the great river of life and counting as losses what God had intended us to count as gain'. He passionately desired that no human talent should ever be wasted. 'My idea of Hell', he once wrote, 'is a place where I won't have any work to do.' And, like Chekhov, he could be 'irritated by the attempts to decry religion'. In this Michael sometimes suffered from his 'friends' who tried to read in him support for their own prejudices and iconoclasms. On the other hand, that brilliant insight, which often led him to discover talent where others had missed it, rarely let him be fooled by the second-rate, the fake or the ambitious man.

Like Eriugena (and indeed Aquinas too) he saw creation as the mirror of God – evil the absence of this reflection. Creatures with choice, men and women, were only what they said they were when they reflected the integrity of the creation in their behaviour. 'When we do violence to our natures . . . we are justified in our regrets.' Truth and Beauty are two different aspects of the same Divinity and beatitude lies at the end of the search for either. He knew 'that there were souls that were immortal, that even God, if He wished to, could not diminish or destroy' and that these 'immortals can forever look at perfect beauty without wearying of it'. But how do mortals become immortal? Man's unaided efforts are not enough. 'Words are finite things and even the loveliest poetry loses its magic in time, even for the man who wrote it, but in this imperfect world it is the nearest we can come to the pleasure of the immortals.' But that daring folly – instilled in his youth – 'had always been with him' since – even *he* might

have a destiny in 'the infinite wastes of eternity'. This innate
instinct for the Good was matched and thus confirmed by the
presence of its opposite, for like Plotinus he believed in an Evil
'haunting this world by necessary law' from which man must
escape.

It seemed like an impasse; it was a problem in which man was
vitally involved, yet all man's efforts led only to the knowledge of
his own ignorance of Reality. Of an early friend Michael wrote:
'We are all trapped, of course, sooner or later, but he was more
inescapably trapped because in him the gap between instinct and
judgment was wider than it is in most of us, and he simply could
not jump it.' Michael jumped it, and like everything else he did
left us in no doubt about how he did it. He found the answer to
the rational impasse in the words of Christ: 'Thou shalt love the
Lord thy God' and 'Thou shalt love thy neighbour.' This was the
pearl of human knowledge. Whatever Reality is, human efforts
can attain it only by following this mandate. 'Christ's reply, if I
understand it, means merely that reality is inapprehensible; that if
we keep our minds and hearts like clear glass, the light of God
shines through us, but that we can be certain of God's presence
within us only by the light it sheds on the world outside us.' The
activity of man in the use of human talent doesn't have to lead
to the appalling rashness of believing in man's ability to earn
immortality, but is countered by a passivity – holding himself
like clear glass – through which God's presence works within
him. Eriugena put it another way: 'Light shines in the darkness of
believing souls, and it shines more and more while, starting from
faith, it tends towards the sight of God.' Common, weak man
could rise to this obviously potential height through the instru-
mentality of the presence of God within him (some call this presence 'Grace') – and this Michael knew to be true because he had
it on the authority of Truth. Life, he said, is an 'allegory to which
you and I belong – the allegory that God knows, the saints live
and the poets expound'. There was a break in the silence and the
terror no longer excluded hope. 'Reality, I suppose, is like that,'

he wrote, 'one looks at it and turns away, appalled by the Gorgon's head. And then one realises that one has lived with it, that one has no other reality than the fact that one has once looked at it with naked eyes and survived.' The violence of the anguished search was mellowed down, but the enthusiasm remained. Tranquillity and peace came with hope, as the first steps to happiness had come with love. There was always the delicate courtesy – the incisive honesty of heart and mind. He was still frightened – and appalled: frightened at a Magnificence so far beyond human understanding, appalled at the puny human ability to respond. The awed fright was visibly present when he served Mass in Auch cathedral some months before he died.

By now his time had almost come. Despite illness that weighed him down, he fought fatigue and still lived with all his heart and soul. There was then a loneliness in his grace and kindness, a noble loneliness that held him remote, even in periods of great pain. From the Psalms he borrowed the expression of his hope: 'I await the resurrection from the dead and eternal life to come.' Of his faith he wrote: 'Perhaps it was the thought of these [the immortals] that turned me finally from poetry to story-telling, to the celebration of those who for me represented all that I should ever know of God. My mother was merely one among them, though, in my human weakness, I valued her most, and now that I am old myself, I remember the line of a psalm (probably mistranslated) that has always been with me since I read it first:

'And when I wake I shall be satisfied with Thy likeness.'

Frank O'Connor at Trinity

PHILIP EDWARDS

Frank O'Connor's speech at the Commencements Dinner at Trinity in the summer of 1962, after he had been given his D.Litt., was not one of his happiest. He gave the impression of being overawed. I suspected he felt himself at the disadvantage which only those who intensely respect learning and have never attended a university can feel. He should have asserted himself for what he was; because most of his listeners were at the disadvantage of respecting artistic creation and not being artists themselves. It is typical of him that he did not so assert himself, but stumbled a little in trying to pay homage to the superiority which he thought to exist in a home of learning.

Yet you would not notice any obvious deference on less formal occasions. I had met him first on Commons earlier that summer when he was David Greene's guest; he had lectured me and challenged me on the authorship of *Edward III* and Marlowe's plays in so positive a way that I, new to it, could only stammer in reply. Though taken aback on this first occasion, I later came rather to approve of this definiteness in matters of delicate scholarship. He had a flair for seeing true problems, and imagination in working out solutions; even if sometimes he seemed demonstrably wrong, the eagerness with which he argued a case did far more for students in bringing seemingly dull and unimportant matters to life than all the measured scholarly caution in the world.

Towards the end of 1962 O'Connor began to talk of offers

which he was receiving from American universities, and I began to wish we could offer him some post in T.C.D. I very much wanted to have a writer associated with the English department; the more I saw of O'Connor, the more I liked and admired him, and I knew that he wanted to stay in Ireland if he could. But Trinity had and has no money to spare on 'luxuries'; for years it has scarcely been able to afford the bare essentials. Obviously we could not compete with American universities, but David Greene encouraged me to try what we could do.

I went to see the Provost, and to my surprise and delight he was immediately interested. 'But, Edwards, wouldn't you think of Sean O'Faolain first?' He knew O'Faolain well and suggested that he had a claim on us as the recipient of an honorary degree long before O'Connor's. This was awkward: in terms of doing something for my department and for College I should have been delighted at the idea of approaching O'Faolain, but at this time I had not met him, and I knew O'Connor and knew that I could work with him and that I wanted to work with him. Anyway, the Provost accepted both the idea and O'Connor, and so did the College officers and so did the Board. I make it sound smoother than it was. It wasn't much of an offer we were allowed to make: £500 for a part-time lectureship.

I had very clear ideas about what I wanted O'Connor to do. When he had accepted Trinity's offer, I realised that *he* had very clear ideas too, and that they weren't in the least like mine. So far as I was concerned, he was the 'writer-in-residence'; he would be a member of the Common Room, use the Library, wander around College, give a class to help those of my students who were trying to write, give some lectures based in some way on his experience as a writer, and give informal help to those of my graduate students who were working on Irish subjects. Except for the last, all this was just what he did not want to do. He had worked himself out in the 'creative-writing class' and in lecturing on the short story in the States. He didn't want to be the tame writer, but an academic lecturer on literature in his own right.

(When I look back at the professional apprehension I felt at letting the amateur O'Connor have his head, I recall an occasion, much later, when we met in College Green and, as we walked up Grafton Street, I told him about an essay I was writing on *The Two Noble Kinsmen* – a play no one reads. I said that the kernel of the play was Emilia's speech about her childhood love for Flavina. I began to grope for the lines I had probably transcribed that morning, but could not get them into my head. We were by the flower-seller at the corner of Duke Street. O'Connor stopped me and stood there and, after a moment's hesitation, declaimed the best part of the speech above the noise of the traffic. His know-ledge of literature really was remarkable.)

We compromised, of course, on what he was to do. He agreed to take the weekly writing class, and I agreed to his giving a weekly lecture on the development of Irish literature from the earliest times to the present day. Later, O'Connor tried to give Greene and me credit for initiating courses in which literature in Irish and in English were treated together. The idea was most certainly O'Connor's. We had a problem about his title. 'Irish literature' meant Gaelic literature; 'Anglo-Irish literature' had specific cultural overtones that ruled it out. It was the Assistant Registrar and not an academic who came up with 'Special Lecturer in the Literature of Ireland'; if it was cumbersome, it was exact and eloquent, and we adopted it. O'Connor bought a gown (which he treasured), and in October 1963 he began his work.

The weekly lectures were immensely successful. My honours students, for whom they had been chiefly intended, never formed more than a fraction of the big audience. The lectures were not public, and they were not advertised, but they soon began to draw in students from University College as well as interested Trinity students whose subjects were anything but literature. Visiting American academics, young writers and unclassifiable members of the public used to drop in. There had been nothing like it since the great days of Dowden's lectures. The 'openness' of the lectures was highly irregular, but of course no one said a word.

O'Connor more or less gave up his year to the preparation of these lectures. He suffered financially and he suffered emotionally. He was always worrying about them. He was nervous before the start of every single lecture. He would come up to my room a quarter of an hour early every Tuesday, and we would talk, with much glancing at watches. Then the donning of gowns and the ritual procession to the lecture-theatre, myself as acolyte with the indispensable flask of water.

Nervous or not, he lectured magnificently. He stood at the lectern, black gown over bright blue tweed jacket, his white head thrown back, reciting in that deep voice his translation of an old Irish poem, reminiscing on something apropos which Yeats had said to him, or dogmatising on matters which made the Celtic scholars from the Institute for Advanced Studies turn and look at each other. He could never understand why at the end there were not more questions. I was always sorry that his own enthusiasm was not repaid by a good discussion. It was better when we reached the Anglo-Irish writers; few of my own students knew anything of Old Irish literature – I think he assumed more knowledge than there was. At any rate, he quite rightly became dissatisfied with a series of lectures attended for their own interest and without any follow-up in the undergraduates' own studies, and he began to think out schemes for degree courses in the literature of Ireland.

We would go back to my room after the lecture. Tom Flanagan from Berkeley (I don't think he missed a lecture) would come with him, and there were always one or two others – Brendan Kennelly, James Carney, Mary Lavin, James Walton and others, and his wife. Relaxed *now*, he'd take charge of the talk, hearty with his admiration or contempt for whatever name came up – he enjoyed strong views. Of his anecdotes, I remember more his tone of voice than the substance: he loved mimicry, and the only thing you could have called malicious about him was his rendering of the accents of Lennox Robinson or Liam O'Flaherty.

I suspect he found his short-story class rather a bore, though he never complained. I well remember how upset he was because a rather trying American student was due to read out his story, which made a good deal of play with the main four-letter word. O'Connor was convinced that the boy was simply out to shock the respectable young Irishwoman of the class. He didn't want to allow the boy his triumph, and at the same time he didn't want to play the censor. It was for him entirely a question of manners and tact. How far the young ladies needed protecting, I can't say, but I was very much struck by the depth of O'Connor's concern, and I have often thought that I only really began to know him from that time. The young man in question came to see me just before one of O'Connor's classes and our conversation made him rather late. At the end of the hour O'Connor called in, smiling broadly and congratulating me on my ingenuity. As the student was not there to read his story at the beginning of the class, he lost his chance for ever; O'Connor would never believe that I had not purposely engineered the delay.

I was to spend 1964–5 in the United States, and David Greene was to be in Israel; O'Connor was not eager to continue in T.C.D. while we were away. When he wrote to the Secretary declining reappointment for 1964–5, he enlarged on what he thought could be the pattern of future developments.

> ... I should be glad if this appointment could be deferred to the following year, partly because I should like to have more time for my own work, but largely because my lectures would not serve the same purpose if delivered in successive years. ... I believe the course will ultimately have to be treated in a more ambitious manner and perhaps widened in scope. ... My own hope would be that the course would be widened in scope and interest by lectures from other members of staff on such closely allied subjects as History, Archaeology and linguistics, and would form the nucleus of a School of Irish Studies that would give the College an assured leadership in this field.

I wrote to the Board in support of this letter and was gratified to get agreement with the proposal to set up a committee to examine O'Connor's proposals. W. B. Stanford, David Greene, Brian Spencer and I were soon busy trying to put the suggestions in practical terms.

We proposed a four-year undergraduate course in Irish literature (i.e. in Irish and English), the Irish language, Irish history, art, culture and sociology. Parts of the course were to serve as a two-year graduate course: an ideal course for the great number of American students applying to do graduate work at T.C.D. Working it out in the most cheese-paring way possible, using existing courses wherever possible, we thought that we could start the scheme with two additional junior staff and one senior person. We presumed that O'Connor, as the 'onlie begetter' would at least get us under way. Everywhere we met interest and approval in our scheme, and we felt the excitement of pioneers in a new academic adventure in Ireland. The Board accepted the proposals, the Provost in particular giving us strong support, and they were put to the Irish government in the annual request for funds. I went off to America, announcing our new programme to everyone.

Back in Ireland, the foreboding that Trinity was going to get very little money from the government grew stronger. The Provost wrote to me that whatever else had to be postponed, Irish Studies would be started. O'Connor wrote to me in February: 'Meanwhile have received two offers of jobs in California ... Do not think I shall receive offer from Trinity. Do not think we will have school of Irish Studies. Do think you had better return, hastily.' There was nothing I could have done, except to find out earlier the news that in a way was kept from me, that the government grant was not sufficient for any new development. It was an intense disappointment to O'Connor, and to me.

When I got back to Ireland, with all our plans defeated, I managed at least to get O'Connor reinstated on the old basis. But his second operation and its (in time fatal) effect prevented his doing more for us than give two public lectures in January 1966 on 'Early Irish Story-Telling'. Before the lecture O'Connor's doctor warned me that he was worried about his heart, but that he was so eager to give the lecture that he could not bring himself to forbid it. The lecture-room was packed. During the whole hour I never took my eyes off O'Connor, and I was flexing my muscles like a slip-fielder in case he collapsed. He was in fact in superb form.

On the Friday before his death he came along to my graduate seminar. He had agreed to let the students ask him about his own work. He was wonderful, and I can still hear him talking. He would never *invent* an incident, he said. Any scrap of conversation which came his way might serve as the germ of a story – if it was enigmatic enough he couldn't rest until he had found circumstances and people which might lead to that scrap of conversation. The core of a story must be for him something that had happened. He told of an American class which was getting nowhere at all with its ideas for stories. 'Go home,' he said to them (it was the Christmas vacation), 'and come back with something odd or amusing that has happened in your family or your neighbours' families.' One girl came back with a superb story of a long-suffering maidservant who had served the Christmas turkey in her outdoor clothes; on carving the bird, they found it had been stuffed with the maid's uniform.

He talked about his trials and errors in fashioning the final versions of some of his best stories. No, he never kept a notebook, and he never recorded dialogue. His stories were all Irish because they all became Irish, no matter where they might have started. No, he never put his friends in his work – he didn't want to hurt them. We talked a lot about the attitude of the writer to using circumstances he was involved in as a person, and this led to deaths and funerals: O'Connor indignantly rejected the idea proffered to him that the true writer could maintain his detachment even at his mother's funeral.

We were never able to give O'Connor the part he wanted to

play in Trinity. He had thrown in his lot with the College, and he had come a long way since he had made that speech at Commencements. He never, perhaps, became so much a part of the place that he'd wander in to lunch without arranging it beforehand, but he became as passionate as an old Trinity hand about what *we* could do that they couldn't or wouldn't do elsewhere in Ireland. So it is all the sadder that he had to watch our plans fail.

He was a wonderful colleague and a wonderful teacher. He had immense patience, and his kindness to individual students was great. The old belief that you cannot be a good writer without being a good man will unfortunately not hold up against the evidence, but when you have a man who was as good a writer and teacher as Frank O'Connor was, you can't help thinking that his goodness as a man had something to do with it.

Poet of the People

DAVID GREENE

There are some figures so simple and so noble that, when we come to talk of them, our own worn-out clichés seem an insult and we have to turn to the enduring words of the past. So, when I think of Frank O'Connor dead and gone from us, the words that come first to me are those of the psalmist: 'The zeal of thy house hath eaten me up . . .'

The zeal was for Ireland, the real Ireland. Not for pietistic frauds, nor for businessmen with an eye to the main chance, nor for pop-song singers: all these he hated, and they repaid him with their hatred: 'They that sit in the gate speak against me; and I was the song of the drunkards.' His love of Ireland began with the land itself, sea and shore, lake and forest: his denunciations of modern despoilers re-echoed the lament for the woods of Cill Chais, which he himself had translated so beautifully.

It was greater still for the works of man in this island, whether the pre-Christian sculptures of the Armagh region, or Ballintubber Abbey, or the Georgian houses of Dublin; nobody knew better than he how little the storms of the centuries have left us, how uncertain our grasp on civilisation. But, since he himself was a master of the word, both written and spoken, his concern was above all with the speech of the people, whether in Irish or English.

He had worked and fought for the Irish language in his youth, knowing that in it lay the key to all but two or three centuries of the history of this nation; in later years he had come to accept

K

reluctantly the decision of the Irish people to reject by their own free will what their fathers had had wrenched from them by famine and oppression. He often spoke, with a mixture of wonder and horror, of the Cork slums of his youth where an old man, too foolish or too senile to conceal his knowledge of the language, was followed round by a pack of louts shouting 'Irish! Irish!'; when the time came, he stood out boldly against the adult analogues of those louts who persecuted his friend the Tailor and who threatened to knock down any memorial stone which might be erected in Feakle graveyard to the memory of Brian Merriman.

Although he learned Irish better than most, he knew that all that was surging in his mind could best be expressed in English, and the rightness of that decision is plain for the world to see. But his zeal for the Irish language remained unabated; if the people had rejected the language itself, he was determined that they should at least be given some notion, even at second hand, of what had existed in it. Not only did he translate widely from modern Irish, but he set himself to master the older language too.

It is as well to understand what this meant. Old Irish is as far from modern Irish as the language of *Beowulf* is from that of the *Daily Mirror*; it is so much more complicated than Old English that even a good honours student, after three or four years at the university, hesitates to tackle a story or poem which he has not been taken over in class. Frank O'Connor had not got beyond the primary school; he was no leisured gentleman sitting in his study, but a selfmade writer who had to live by his pen, so that the time spent on learning Old Irish represented so many guineas or dollars unearned.

But he learned it, and learned it well, so well that he won the respect of scholars as critical as Daniel Binchy and Calvert Watkins. Not because he was their equal in discussing etymologies and grammatical forms – he wasn't and he didn't try to be – but because Old Irish was to him the means of understanding so much about the Irish people, and because he brought to it the intuition of the supreme craftsman. He knew why people wrote stories and poems, and that is an aspect of the matter that the professional scholars have not concerned themselves very much with.

Some people learn for their own private satisfaction, others for the pleasure of displaying their erudition; to Frank O'Connor such attitudes were incomprehensible. He had learned the older language so that he could tell the Irish people about it; after reading a poem that had especially moved him he would look up and say: 'Isn't it grand? Think how the kids down the country would love that!' He infected me so much with his enthusiasm that I fell in with his project of producing an anthology of the earlier poetry, which he did not live to see published; the printing of the original Irish is no scholarly ostentation, but derives from Frank O'Connor's entirely unaffected belief that if he could understand it any kid down the country could so as well. He believed in the Irish people.

Most of all he believed in the young. His love for students was unbounded. And he was, quite literally, inspired when he lectured to young people; he gathered up all that he had ever felt and learned and poured it out in front of them.

Politics, aesthetics, teaching, controversy – are these any part of the duty of a creative artist? No, but they are part of the duty of the full man, of the zealous man, and they ate up Frank O'Connor before his time. He would not have chosen it otherwise.

Frank O'Connor and the *New Yorker*

WILLIAM MAXWELL

A poet friend whose literary judgment I greatly respected told me
to read a book of short stories called *Crab Apple Jelly*, by an Irish
writer named Frank O'Connor, and I did. Shortly afterward I
met him – by accident, I think – in the office of the man who at
that time was his editor at the *New Yorker*. His voice was the
thing I noticed above everything else. As a rule when I am being
introduced to a man or woman who interests me, I am so intent
on searching the eyes I don't even hear what they are saying, let
alone the quality of the voice. Michael's I heard with astonish-
ment. I am grateful that it is there on the records he made and
gave me, but I don't need to go to the record player to find out
what his voice sounded like. I hear it whenever I think of him.
And it is that as much as anything that keeps me from being able
to accept the fact that he is dead.

His voice, his face, his innocent nature, his knowledge of the
world – these come to mind not in any order of importance; they
are just part of the way I remember him. I was aware of them all
during that first meeting. Also of something else: he seemed to be
talking to me and looking at me as if he liked me. On sight.
Nothing that I learned about him later has ever suggested that he
was cautious in getting to know people or about the people he
got to know, though he was, I have been told, sometimes concerned about what might happen to the people who got to know
him.

His clothes; those rough Harris tweed coats. The smell of his pipe tobacco. His smile. His kindness. There is a snapshot of him that I keep under the glass top of my desk – taken in Vermont, on the front porch of a white clapboard house. He is addressing a raccoon. Their size being very different, Michael is bending from the hips in what looks rather like a formal bow, and from the way the fingers of his right hand are arranged he is either offering the raccoon a morsel of food or making an important literary distinction. The raccoon is balancing on his hind legs, his nose lifted as high as it will go, his gaze earnestly directed not at the food (if it is food) but at Michael's face. He is, obviously, head over heels in love. No human being has ever bothered to understand him before, and the understanding of other raccoons is not the thing he has needed all his life. What is also clear from the snapshot is that the affection is reciprocated. Without this blaze of understanding, which he had hardly dared hope for and perhaps no longer expected to find, that raccoon might well have perished. The conversation is not in words but direct from the heart, one creature to another.

His voice, his face. The horn-rimmed glasses. The eyes that, when I try to recall them exactly, give me trouble; their color varies all the way from hazel to a brown so dark that it seems black, and this cannot have been possible. It can only be an effect of distance. The thick gray hair and the gray mustache. The fiery black eyebrows. The color of his skin, and the habitual lines of his face, in his forehead, at the corners of the eyes particularly, and bracketing his mouth. Though he was not free from worry, it didn't show. The lines expressed only animation, the mind excited by and delighting in perceptiveness. To say that someone's voice is like a musical instrument, or like a bell, is not in the least accurate; you are describing the effect and not the thing itself. But Michael's voice did have, did suggest, the quality of reverberation and, compared to the flat and toneless way that Americans speak, it was musical. The Irish accent (unlike the English) often strikes Americans as enchanting, but I have never met an Irishman whose voice reminded me of Michael's. Speech being learned by imitation, no doubt his took its quality and timbre from the voices he heard in earliest childhood. How he used it was something else again – one of the innumerable gifts he appears to have been born with, like the ability to teach himself a language, and that most people do not have.

Though it is quite true, as one hears said, that we are the sum of all that has happened to us, the converse is equally true: before anything whatever has happened to us we are something, and we continue to be that something all the rest of our lives. If you don't believe me, look at the photograph in *An Only Child* which bears the caption 'Minnie O'Donovan and the author aged four months'. If that baby suddenly began to explain just how the Casement diaries have been tampered with, or said, 'Even from its beginnings, the short story has functioned in a quite different way from the novel', I wouldn't turn a hair. It is so unmistakably himself, half buried in lace and a white bunting, and squirming with discomfort at having to sit for the photographer. As for the woman, she died before I ever knew Michael, but I was present during the period in which he was engaged in bringing her back to life.

He came to my office frequently during those months when he was writing and the *New Yorker* was publishing a large part of the first volume of his autobiography. The moment of his arrival I can re-enact at will. The shape in the doorway, the smile of delighted greeting, the big wool tam-o'-shanter – the only tam-o'-shanter in the whole city of New York – the voice speaking my name, and the envelope in his hand, containing manuscript. We sat at a table, with the manuscript spread out in front of us or with galleys embroidered with queries from the proofreader, and talked. His conversation was so easy, so broad-ranging, so without vanity or suspicion. And he was so quick to sense what can and what cannot be talked about. When we had wandered far enough afield, we would come back to the work at hand. Directing his attention to this or that place on the page, was all there that the situation had in it, I would ask. Was this word right? Was that sentence what he really meant? Did he need to say that? Wasn't it implied? And weren't there too many adverbs describing how the characters said what they said? And so on. Finicky laboring away at the surface of the writing. And he embraced this new game (or perhaps it was not new; he may have run across the disease of perfectionism before this) with the enthusiasm and receptivity of a big friendly sheep dog. It was not, of course, where his heart lay at all. Probably he was just being polite, though it may have interested him; all sorts of things did. But left to himself, he would not have been putting his mind to these matters. In the course of an interview published in the *Paris Review* in the fall of 1957, he was asked the question 'How do you start a story?' and answered,

'Get black on white', used to be Maupassant's advice – that's what I always do. I don't give a hoot what the writing's like; I write any sort of rubbish which will cover the main outlines of the story, then I can begin to see it. When I write, when I draft a story, I never think of writing nice sentences . . . I just write roughly what happened, and then I'm able to see what the construction looks like. It's the design of the story which to me is most important, the thing that tells you there's a bad gap in the narrative here and you really ought to fill that up in some way or another. I'm always looking at the design of a story, not the treatment.

You cannot say that the man who wrote 'The engine shrieked; the porter slammed the door with a curse; somewhere another door opened and shut, and the row of watchers, frozen into effigies of farewell, now dark now bright, began to glide gently past the window, and the stale, smoky air was charged with the breath of open fields' was indifferent to which word he used, or to the shape of his sentences. Or that he wasn't, indeed, a poet. But in the main it is true – style wasn't his besetting preoccupation. He had it, and he used it, like any other tool of his trade. It was the design he worked at – the design and one other thing. In that same interview he says:

. . . if you're the sort of person that meets a girl in the street and instantly notices the color of her eyes and of her hair and the sort of dress she's wearing, then you're not in the least like me. I just notice a feeling from people. I notice particularly the cadence of their voices, the sort of phrases they'll use, and that's what I'm all the time trying to hear in my head, how people word things – because everybody speaks in an entirely different language, that's really what it amounts to. I have terribly sensitive hearing and I'm terribly aware of voices. If I remember somebody, for instance, that I was very fond of, I don't remember what he or she looked like, but I can absolutely take off the voice. I'm a good mimic; I've a bit of the actor in me, I suppose, that's really what it amounts to. I cannot pass a story as finished unless I can act it myself – unless I know how everybody in it spoke . . . If I use the right phrase and the reader hears the phrase in his head, he sees the individual . . .

It used to amuse and interest him that when we were considering an early draft of a story together, I would ask what the furniture was like, or what the inside of the house looked like. 'Oh, Lord,' he would exclaim, 'don't ask me that!' And he couldn't, in fact, tell me. He was not interested in interior decoration. If he was writing a story, he would place a house in its street, and that street in its surroundings, and then he would do the front garden, and then, having delivered the reader at the front door he went blind at the very moment the door was opened, because now there were people, and the people were talking, and it was a matter of getting the voices right.

A sudden doubt about the correctness of what I have been saying sent me to the bookcase, and I re-read 'The Man of the World', a story in which an interior figures importantly. This is what I found:

At that moment a faint light became visible in the great expanse of black wall: a faint yellow stair light that was just sufficient to silhouette the window frame below us. Suddenly the whole room lit up. The man I had seen in the street stood by the doorway, his hand still on the switch. I could see it all plainly now – an ordinary small, suburban bedroom with flowery wallpaper, a colored picture of the Sacred Heart over the double bed with the big brass knobs, a wardrobe, and a dressing table.

So he could do it when he needed to. And in a way that was masterly. But linger over the details he did not. That's all the description there is. From there on, the focus is entirely on the characters.

Fiction can and often does deal seriously with ideas, but it is not really fiction at all unless the ideas are embodied in believable characters. Evelina, Lord Belmont's daughter, Pip and Joe and Miss Havisham and Estella and the convict. The reader must be able to identify himself with the characters and care what happens to them or the book falls from his hands of its own weight. It is conceivable that in order for a writer to be able to deal with human beings in an imaginative way he must at some time have been deeply and wholly committed to *a* character – someone large enough and important enough to come between him and the light of common day. Which brings us back to the photograph on page 87 of *An Only Child*:* Minnie O'Donovan in a dress of striped silk, with a silk scarf pinned at her throat, and one of those boat-shaped hats women wore at the turn of the century, trimmed with an ostrich feather. The thin face, the brave, purposeful, beautiful eyes, the sensitive mouth. The orphan who was driven to the brink of suicide by misfortune and unkindness, the figure that all through his childhood came between Michael and whatever was unbearable. The air he breathed. The climate of love. If you have tears to shed, read the page that faces that picture and you will shed them.

Stature has to come from somewhere, just like the color of eyes and hair, the shape of hands, mouth and nose, the timbre of the voice. His, one can only suppose, came from her. Because of her the relationship one entered into when one became his friend was totally without smallness. He did not say, 'There is nothing I would not do for you,' he merely bided his time and eventually demonstrated that this was so. And for all the essential innocence of his nature, he did not, I think, become friends with people he could not in some way admire. ('There is only one man in each

* Cf. American Edition.

town one can learn from, and he's always moving. I told you many times about Binchy ... Now he's got a professorship in Harvard.') Even those friendships that did not last out the lives of the two people involved – for example, his friendship with Daniel Corkery – had about them a kind of afterglow, a light and warmth that time had no effect on. He put Corkery's best novel in my hands and insisted that I read it. He made me forever aware of Corkery's gifts as a writer, as a teacher. Sometimes I even catch myself thinking that Corkery was *my* friend.

An only child, Michael behaved as if he were the oldest of a large family of boys and girls. With patience and good humor he put up with a great many things that were not to his liking. Not bullying, though. The size of the bully was something he measured accurately, but with one part of his mind only, the detached part, that had no control over his actions. Now I *am* in for it, he remarked to himself and rushed into the fray, to defend the weak, the timid, the defenceless. The defamed dead. The misunderstood. Though he made fun of himself as the defender of the weak, I never saw anyone push him around.

He did not go in for being an important writer, though he was one; or an important anything. Writing was what mattered to him. The fascination of it. The difficulties. The happiness of getting it down right. The whole area in which artists, in their absorption and singlemindedness, are like solitary children playing with building blocks or crayons or clay. In his case it was black on white. He was an original and I think first-rate literary critic. What he could honestly praise he praised. And he did not require you to praise him. '. . . this isn't even supposed to be a story but a piece of pure lyricism in which the characters are regarded merely as voices in a bit of instrumental music. It's one of the odd things I do for my own satisfaction, without expecting anybody in the world to like it except myself.' Very often he spoke as if the idea or the experience out of which the story came about had itself somehow done the writing, while he stood by and watched. Cuts, transposition of sentences, rewording of phrases, all tinkering of this kind he accepted enthusiastically; so much so that sometimes, having made a suggestion, one then had to turn around and protect him from a too quick and unconsidered acceptance of it. When we were finished he would carry me off to look at a neglected church or to pay a visit to some bookstore. Or, as if we were schoolboys, I must go home with him. If I could have stopped him from going back to Ireland to live I would have.

When I had his friendship I tried to make the most of it. When he went back to Ireland I tried to go on being his editor, but the Atlantic Ocean came between us. Letters are not the same as sitting down at a table with manuscript and galleys spread out in front of you and saying whatever comes into your mind. Stories he felt were entirely successful I could not like. And he was ill. 'Bill doesn't love me any more,' he said to Harriet.

When I think of him I hear his voice, I see his extraordinary face, I remember the affectionate and amused expression in his eyes, the kingly turn of the head, the beautiful smile. In speaking of him I cannot bring myself to use the past tense.

The Irish Writer

THOMAS FLANAGAN

In 1964, on the night before my return to America, I saw Frank O'Connor – my friend Michael O'Donovan – for the last time. We took a walk which we made twice a week, across Baggot Street Bridge and down the broad Georgian streets of Dublin's vanished gentility toward the mountains which rose darkly at the end of each prospect. A wide circle carried us to a favorite pub of his, one which Dublin's lilliputian version of the affluent society had not tarted-up as a 'lounge', and finally, an hour or so later, we recrossed the bridge.

I have almost forgotten the topics of that night's conversation. His enthusiasms and aversions were numerous and intense – James Joyce, eighth-century Ireland, Chekhov, Jane Austen, pedants, the present Abbey Theatre, public figures foreign and domestic, the Church, professional patriots, the 'forged' (as he believed them) Casement diaries, manuscripts and old books, eighteenth-century Ireland, the Board of Censorship, compulsory Gaelic, the ruined abbeys of Connaught and Munster, his native city of Cork, Celtophobes and Celtophiles, schools which mistreated children, the operas of Mozart. My role, I had discovered, was to offer unrelenting dissent, no light task when walking full-tilt: in his youth, as a member of the Irish Republican Army, he had spent months on the run, and had never really slowed down. Moreover, he could argue any issue with the wiles of Odysseus, and his brief, vivid rages were magnificent. 'He was like a man who takes a machine-gun to a shooting gallery,' Sean O'Faolain has written. 'Everybody falls flat on his face, the proprietor at once takes to the hills, and when it is all over, and you cautiously peep up, you find that he has wrecked the place but got three perfect bull's-eyes.'

But the conversation, whether in New York or California or Dublin, had a way of turning to Ireland, and Ireland was somehow at issue as we recrossed the bridge. Some final and doubtless conclusive point occurred to him, and he paused to drive it home. Baggot Street Bridge arches over the eighteenth-century canal which once carried travellers across the midland bogs and green fields to the Shannon. Its Dublin reaches, at least, retain traces of loveliness. Trees line the double tow-paths on either side, a great convenience and protection to lovers: 'The trees along the canal', it has been remarked, 'are more sinned against than sinning.' Swans often float on the waters between the narrow locks, cutting and breaking the clear reflections of claret-colored Georgian houses. As it happened, the canal was yet another of Michael's concerns: it had recently been suggested that if filled and cemented over, it would make a splendid car-park, with an auxiliary sewer running underneath. He now interrupted himself to discuss this matter in forceful language, but paused in the midst of the new discourse, having noticed, with incredulous anger, that I was laughing. I could find no way to explain that it was the laughter of admiration and affection.

He was an impressive man – tall and erect, with the head of an old king, piercing brown eyes behind glasses, a shock of white hair and a bristling mustache. When he argued, the great handsome head was thrown back imperiously, and the effect was likely to daunt the most seasoned debater. Seeing him thus, his back to the water and dark hills, I was struck once again by the fact of his life-long lover's quarrel with his country. Like Yeats and Joyce and O'Casey, he had long ago decided that Ireland was morally bound to live up to expectations he had formed in youth. The absurd Stephen Dedalus tells Bloom that 'Ireland may be important because it belongs to me'. And Yeats laments that he has too often been tempted from his craft of verse by 'the seeming needs of my fool-driven land'. Frank O'Connor lacked the arrogance needed for such assertions, but not the pride from which they issued. 'Europe's sleeping-beauty sister', as he somewhere calls her, needed a stern talking-to every so often, and there were several lengthy trial-separations, but he always returned to resume his maddened and at times maddening exhortations. 'I prefer', he once wrote, 'to write about Ireland and Irish people merely because I know to a syllable how everything in Ireland can be said.' The modesty of that 'merely' is deceitful: Joyce would have recognized the pride of craft and place which it implies.

He wrote close to a hundred short stories, of which a full score at least – including 'Guests of the Nation', 'In the Train', 'Uprooted', 'The Luceys', 'The Mad Lomasneys', 'The Step-Mother', 'The Holy Door', 'The Masculine Principle' – seem to me as fine as any in our literature. But in Ireland it will be a while before his work is properly appreciated, and, again as with Yeats, precisely because the personality was as vivid and strong as the work is distinguished. The singular adventures, spiritual and public, out of which the literature of modern Ireland issued, made of its greatest writers exemplary figures, arguing within their art and outside it the meaning of the Irish experience. But now Ireland has joined our common world, and hopes to join its common market, and there may no longer be room or need for a writer like O'Connor.

Guests of the Nation (1931) is the work of a young man who had been drawn out of one of the worst slums in Cork by the guerrilla war against England. Its title story, stark and terrible, must be known to most readers of modern fiction. Two British soldiers, 'Awkins and Belcher, are being held hostage against the impending execution of rebel prisoners. Guards and hostages become friends – Donovan, Noble and the unnamed narrator; 'Awkins, the perky little Cockney, his head crammed with Sunday-newspaper radicalism; Belcher, the sweet-tempered, slow-moving Tommy.

> I couldn't at the time see the point of me and Noble being with Belcher and 'Awkins at all, for it was and is my fixed belief you could have planted that pair in any untended spot from this to Claregalway and they'd have stayed put and flourished like a native weed. I never seen in my brief experience two men that took to the country like they did. . . . 'Awkins told me he learned to dance 'The Walls of Limerick' and 'The Siege of Ennis' and 'The Waves of Troy' in a night or two, though naturally he could not return the compliment, because our lads at that time did not dance foreign dances on principle.

But the sentences against the rebels in the distant city are carried out, and Donovan brings word from Brigade that the hostages are to be shot in reprisal. 'Awkins responds with voluble and angry fear, but not Belcher:

> 'You understand,' says Jeremiah Donovan, 'it's not so much our doing. It's our duty, so to speak.' Belcher's head is raised like a real blind man's, so that you can only see his nose and chin in the lamp-light. 'I never could make out what duty was myself,' he said, 'but I think you're all good lads, if that's what you mean. I'm not complaining.' Noble, with a look of desperation, signals to Donovan, and in a flash Donovan raises his gun and fires. The big man goes over like a sack of meal, and this time there is no need of a second shot.

Belcher, stoic and skeptic, is not alone in his doubts; the narrator is left for ever with his memory of the patch of black bog with the two Englishmen stiffening into it. But the story's power issues directly from the narrator's refusal to speculate beyond the needs of the occasion. His offhand remark about foreign dances is almost the only reference to the cause which had brought his bannerless army into being. O'Connor was later to say that the stories of revolution which make up the volume were influenced by the example of Isaac Babel. And they do employ Babel's great feat of juxtaposing violence and repose, action and vision.

But there, in technique, the resemblance ends. The aesthetics of violence held little appeal for O'Connor; quite the contrary, in fact. Jo Kiely, the 'latter-end man' in another story, develops skill and zest in killing, and thus shocks the narrator: 'On those very words we parted, and somehow I could never bring myself to be pally with Jo again. Though, as I said before, he was an imaginary man, and didn't always mean what he said, there was a terrible wild streak in him. And after that, too, I never spoke a word to Jo's girl again.'

O'Connor was responding to a similarity between his situation and Babel's – young slum intellectuals swept into revolutions which overturned their societies and their inner worlds, the bookish and bespectacled companions of violent men. But Babel, in his wonderful phrase, fought with autumn in his heart, whereas revolutionary Ireland, with its ambushes and Mills bombs and home-made artillery, was for O'Connor a springtime world. Characteristically, the stories are not sober but comic, and this is particularly true of those written out of his own experiences, as with the story of the shopkeeper who acquires a machine-gun from the departing British and sets out to sell his services, impartially, to Free Staters and Republicans. Again and again we catch glimpses of young Michael O'Donovan. In 'Laughter': 'Now, one night Alec had a private ambush – quite unorthodox, like everything he did. He launched a bomb at a lorry of soldiers in the street, and then ran away up a dark lane, his cap pulled well down over his eyes, and his hand on the butt of his revolver.' In 'The Patriarch': 'Lounging round street corners, cap pulled over my eyes, hands in pockets, being smacked or kicked about by policemen, reporting at night to someone in Michael's little shop – oh, it was all thrilling and wonderful!'

But a darker thread also runs through the stories, connecting them and carrying us to what was to remain a center of his moral vision – a detestation of the abstract, of abstraction as it acts upon and against character. What properly impressed him about the revolution was what he came to call its 'imaginative' quality – its

improvisation, gaiety and make-believe. A few thousand farm-
boys and clerks, ill-armed but resourceful, had set themselves up
against an empire. But the springtime revolution was followed by
the heartbreaking and far more deadly Civil War. O'Connor
served with the intransigent Republicans against the moderate
Free State and its Treaty, but the stories of civil war display little
partisan feeling. The Republicans are usually 'our side', and the
Free Staters 'the other chaps'. But the autobiographical *An Only
Child* (1961) expresses deep, if evenly divided bitterness, and one
passage deserves quotation at length:

> But meanwhile the improvisation had cracked: the English could
> have cracked it much sooner merely by yielding a little to it.
> When, after election results had shown that a majority of the
> people wanted the compromise – and when would *they* not have
> accepted a compromise? – our side continued to maintain that the
> only real government was the imaginary one, or the few shadowy
> figures that remained of it, we were acting on the unimpeachable
> logic of the imagination, that only what exists in the mind is real.
> What we ignored was that a whole section of the improvisation
> had cut itself adrift and become a new and more menacing reality.
> ... Rory O'Connor and Mellowes in seizing the Four Courts
> were merely echoing Patrick Pearse and the seizure of the Post
> Office, and Michael Collins, who could so easily have starved
> them out with a few pickets, imitated the English pattern by
> blasting the Four Courts with borrowed artillery. And what
> neither group saw was that every word we said, every act we
> committed, was a destruction of the improvisation and what we
> were bringing about was a new Establishment of Church and
> State in which improvisation would play no part, and young men
> and women would emigrate to the ends of the earth, not because
> the country was poor but because it was mediocre.

'We had fed the heart on fantasies,' Yeats wrote of these years.
'The heart's grown brutal from the fare.' As an explanation of
recent Irish history, that paragraph is more ingenious than en-
lightening. Fanaticism, after all, is often the dark twin of imaginative politics. And if Ireland really did, as he argues, settle for

L

mediocrity, this may be because in human affairs mediocrity is often the only available alternative to violence and improvisation. The Irish Revolution was probably the last rebellion to be fought along old-fashioned, romantic lines, with ample room for personal enterprise and with aspirations drawn from the rich nineteenth-century storehouse of liberal belief. Its melancholy aftermath was born in the heady years of its early triumphs.

The old 'Patriarch' in one of the loveliest of the early stories is a small shopkeeper who has spent long decades dreaming of rebellion and worshipping, from a safe distance, the Gaelic language. One day the boy who is narrating the story recites for him a verse in Gaelic learned from his slovenly and dirty grandmother. 'I'd give five years of my life to learn it,' the shopkeeper cries. 'The kings and priests and prophets of our race are speaking to us out of the mouths of children, and they might as well be speaking to that counter there.' The boy obligingly offers his grandmother's translation: 'O, my wife and my children and my little spinning-wheel. My couple of pounds of flax each day not spun – two days she's in bed for one she's around the house, and O, may the dear God help me to get rid of her.' The patriarch is taken aback by the swift descent from glorious sound to Blarney Street reality, but he retreats in good order: 'Believe me, there's a message in that you and I don't see. They wrapped their meanings in dark words to deceive their enemies. . . . Dark songs for a people in chains.'

O'Connor himself, his generation and the one preceding it are the butts of that story. A vision, not far distant from the 'Patriarch's', of Ireland and of Irish possibilities had drawn him away from the series of ugly cottages in which he was reared. His first memories were of a cottage in Blarney Lane, 'which begins at the foot of Shandon Street, near the river-bank, in sordidness, and ascends the hill toward something like squalor'. A road beyond, near where the country began, led to the Good Shepherd Convent, where his mother had grown up in the orphanage, and at the foot of Convent Avenue was the house where for eight years she had worked as maid. At the other end of Blarney Street, a bridge crossed the Lee to Douglas Street, where an uncle had a cobbler's shop. That was the respectable side of the family. His father was an ex-soldier, an unreliable laborer, an habitual drunkard. The grandmother, 'huge, shiftless, and dirty', was a perpetual embarrassment to the young boy when, at his mother's urging, he set about to better himself.

He owed much to his mother, with her hard, sweet pride and natural gentility of mind and character, and in the autobiography the debt is acknowledged with a moving openness of sentiment. His other early debt was to Daniel Corkery, the gifted but severely limited writer and scholar who drifted to Cork to serve as schoolmaster. For O'Connor, as for other young Irish intellectuals, it was Corkery, rather than Yeats, who opened the gateway to that Gaelic culture which, hidden and half-outlawed, had survived beside the dominant Anglo-Irish one. On the first page of his *Threshold of Quiet* (1917), Corkery takes us from the busy streets of Cork, 'the flat of the city', up the wide-sweeping, treeless, cloud-shadowed hills to the countryside beyond – and this might be taken to define his mission both as writer and as publicist. The Anglo-Irish war was fought in the streets of Dublin and Cork on behalf of the distant hills and lakes of Connaught and Munster. But Corkery was also, as O'Connor was to discover in the course of their revolutionary association, a fiercely sectarian nationalist, his allegiance given in equal parts to an improbable past and an impossible future. The autobiography describes with care and tact O'Connor's estrangement from his literary and political mentor, as he watched Corkery harden, but in conversation he was more terse. One day I told him that I had bought a copy of Corkery's *Hounds of Banba* on the quays for sixpence: 'You were robbed,' he growled.

O'Connor's insistence on the decline of the Civil War from romantic protest to murderous fantasy was given strength by his own singular experience. By the spring of 1923 it had become clear to him that both the foes and the friends of the invisible

Republic – its president, perhaps appropriately, was a mathematician – were going mad. Corkery and he had recently been consulting a celebrated virago of the revolution as to the propriety of shooting women from ambush. 'You seem to have some moral objection to killing women,' she said disapprovingly. He admitted that he had. He was not greatly disturbed, therefore, when Free State soldiers scooped him up one day and shipped him to detention barracks outside Dublin.

Strict Republican discipline was of course maintained within the barracks, a situation put to the test at one point by a man named Murphy, who disobeyed his hut-leader, was courtmartialled, and was placed in a prison-within-the-prison, a shack borrowed by the Republicans from their own Free State captors. Murphy promptly went on hunger-strike, to the embarrassment of his colleagues, who were planning a massive hunger-strike of their own on orders from Headquarters. Even the diehard I.R.A., which had by this time developed elaborate systems of metaphysical jugglery, found the situation unnerving, as though a band of medieval nominalists had awakened one morning to find every pin occupied by three angels. Their ingenious solution was to release but then boycott him; of some nine hundred prisoners, only one voted in the negative. 'Later in life,' he was to say, 'I realized that it was probably the first time I had taken an unpopular stand.'

It was O'Connor himself, with one ally, who held out against the mass hunger-strike, presumably in the name of common sense. It was a remarkable act of moral independence on the part of a young man of twenty, an act which thrust him into opposition not to the British nor to the Free State, but to men whose ideals he still shared and whose friendship he valued. The chapter in which he describes it is admirable in tone, poised between gravity and gaiety, the account of a mutiny carried out without heroics and without sacrifice of his Irish ability to have a good time in jail. And yet something essential is being withheld from the reader. A story of his called 'Jerome' opens (in its first version) this way:

'There are some people so cautious I wonder they ever let themselves get born. Cork people in particular; if caution was transmitted instead of acquired that place would be depopulated long ago.' He knew whereof he spoke, and Cork caution often deploys itself behind an engaging air of reckless candor. The moral center which spurred him to that remarkable act of independence fed upon sources which the autobiography, a book of many concealed reticences, does not suggest.

At any event, when he was released and sent home a year later, his character had found its mould: 'But on the following Sunday I found I did not want to go to Mass, and at the first and only political meeting I attended, Corkery had to rescue me from a young man who called me a traitor. After that, it was friends who believed I had done wrong in opposing the hunger strike, and a girl who said bitterly when I met her in the street: "I hear you don't believe in God any longer."' The autobiography closes with that episode, a Cork street-scene which may well have found its way into the stories. Into 'The Mortal Coil', for example: 'Every Sunday morning, at a time when the rest of the city was at church, a few of us met down the quays. We ranged from a clerical student with scruples to a roaring atheist. The atheist, Dan Turner, was the one I liked best.'

Decades later, when he was making a selection from his volumes of tales, he included from *Guests of the Nation* only a revised version of the title story, and only three stories from *Bones of Contention* (1936), its successor. It was a needless sacrifice of some excellent tales, and the book of selections, by slighting the first ten years of his creative life, does not give a balanced view either of his development or of his range of interests. But perhaps he was right in thinking that with *Crab Apple Jelly* (1944), and in such stories as 'The Luceys' and 'The Mad Lomasneys' he came most fully into possession of his manner and his subject. 'They describe for the first time', he was to say, 'the Irish middleclass Catholic way of life with its virtues and its faults without any of the picturesqueness of early Irish writing which concentrated on color and extravagance.'

Ireland, middleclass and Catholic, is a formidable instance of the closed society. Anthropologists squander their time frivolously by concentrating on islands afloat on more exotic seas. And O'Connor, when he takes us into those mahogany parlors in Sunday's Well, persuades us with the finality of art that we are entering that world, with its unspoken alliances and feuds, its pieties and evasions, its cautious and caustic pronouncements. Some of the stories are harsh and some display a deliberately casual brutality as they unfold lives wasted within a society which is both nurturing and oppressive.

It is a substantial, dowdy and unbreakably provincial world of publicans, doctors, priests, small merchants, builders, chemists and solicitors. And its inhabitants live desperate but never quiet lives in which pubs, conversation and romantic illusion offer, in their various ways, unavailing solace. And their histories are set down with such humor and verve that the melancholy depths are not visible, so that the conclusions, though inevitable, come with a wrench. What is most remarkable (remarkable, that is, for our day) is that the stories are set down without a shade of condescension; the narrator always identifies himself as part of that society, even when he laughs at it or rebels against it. To be sure, when he plays favorites or chooses sides, he is always on the side of spirit, imagination and fire. Rita Lomasney, returning in disgrace from her schoolteaching job, is clearly a favorite:

'Anyway,' she went on, 'he told his old one he wanted to chuck the Church and marry me. There was ructions, of course. The people in the shop at the other side of the street had a son a priest. His old one thought they'd never live down the scandal. So away with her up to the Rev. and the Rev. sends for me. Did I want to destroy the young man's life and he on the threshold of a great calling? I said 'twas they wanted to destroy him. "What sort of priest would he make?" said I. Oh, 'twas a marvellous sacrifice to be called to make, and after it he'd be twice the man. Honest to

God, Ned, the way she went on you'd think she was talking about doctoring an old tomcat. "He will like fun," says I. "That's all you know about Tony." "Oh, we know him well," says the Rev. "He was the altar boy here." "Did he ever tell ye the way he used to slough the convent orchard and sell the apples in town?" says I. So, begor, then she dropped the Holy Willie stuff and told me his ma was after getting into debt to put him in for the priesthood. Three hundred quid! Wouldn't they kill you with style?'

He was right about his talent: he knew to a syllable how everything could be said in Ireland. He knew how an Irish story should open:

Old Myles Reilly in our town was a building contractor in a small way of business that would never be any larger owing to the difficulty of doing sums, but to make up for that he was a great hand at daughters. He had three of them, all stunners; yet he continued to lament the sons he never had, although there was hardly a schoolboy in the town who didn't raise his cap to him as if he was the priest, partly in reverence, partly in the hope of impressing his spotty visage on the old man's mind so that one day he might say to one of the daughters 'Who is that charming fellow from St. Joseph's Terrace? Best-mannered boy in the locality – why don't we have him here to tea some night?' Mind you, there was no recorded instance of Reilly saying anything like that, which might be as well, for if the small boys' mothers didn't actually imply that the girls were fast, they made no bones about saying that they were flighty and needed some respectable woman to put manners on them. Small boys' mothers are like that.

'Old Myles Reilly in our town . . .' The operative word is 'our', which controls the tone of the paragraph. In none of O'Connor's stories is it 'their' town, and the stories are never about what 'they' are doing. The narrative voice comes from deep within the society, the amused, tolerant and sardonic voice of a man commenting on his neighbors and his world. The many re-writings and revisions were devoted to the creation of just that illusion. 'Generations of skilful stylists', he has written, 'from Chekhov to Katherine Mansfield and James Joyce had so fashioned the short story that it no longer rang with the tone of a man's voice, speaking.' He may well have been wrong in supposing that the short story has been robbed of narrative impulse – his critical opinions were invariably sweeping – but entirely right in supposing that the narrator's voice was at the exact center of his own art. It was through the cultivation of that voice that he worked out his complicated relationship to his land and his fellow-countrymen.

There is a striking passage in the autobiography. Republican resistance has ended, and there is a fall in morale within the prison:

> We knew we should never again find ourselves with so many men we respected and we felt their humiliation as though it were our own. In the years to come, travelling through the country, I would meet with the survivors of the period – some of the best, like Walsh, I should not meet because they took off early for America. 'The Lost Legion' I called them. There they were in small cities and towns, shopkeepers or civil servants, bewildered by the immensity of the disaster that had overwhelmed them, the death-in-life of the Nationalist Catholic establishment, and after a few minutes I would hear the cry which I had so often heard before – 'The country! Oh, God, the bloody country!'

Within a very few years, the ex-Republicans were happily – and successfully – competing for the fruits of office against their recent captors.

Nevertheless that passage does speak to the feelings of the Republican intellectuals as they surveyed their uncompleted revolution and their unchanged land. Irish fiction of the period is the record of their responses – the novels of Sean O'Faolain and Liam O'Flaherty and Francis Stuart. And, in a most indirect way, the work of Frank O'Connor. O'Connor, reflecting as a young man upon the meaning of his experience, wonders 'if I should ever again be completely at ease with this people I loved, their introverted religion and their introverted politics'. And it may be that only in his stories did he ever find that ease. 'Frank O'Connor,' Benedict Kiely once said, 'can be as outrageously at ease with his own people as a country parish priest skelping the courting couples out of the ditches. That is one of the ironies of Ireland and of Irish fiction and of Frank O'Connor.'

He said of himself, in an early poem:

> Last Sunday morning,
> Sitting on the tram,
> I found myself beside a priest,
> A fat and gloomy man,
> I looked over his shoulder,
> And I read namquam.
> Now I happened to be reading,
> Les Amours de Madame,
> And even though he scowled at me,
> I didn't give a damn,
> And that just shows you
> The sort I am.

It does indeed, but it also adds another to Kiely's list of ironies. From prison-camp and from the hillsides of armed men, O'Connor carried away a rebelliousness and an independence which served him well as an artist yet inevitably served to separate him from the people among whom he was so outrageously at home. The terms of separation are clearer in works other than the tales. *Irish Miles* (1947), a lighthearted book of travel and architecture, is alive with the bravado and the careless erudition which captivated and at times enraged his friends. But beneath the lightheartedness is a bitterness expressed more subtly in the stories. Talking with a shopkeeper near Slievenamon, an intelligent and disappointed man, he thinks: 'I shall never forget the picture of him in shirt-sleeves at the gate; himself and the woman, she with her loneliness, he with his frustration, symbols of all the inhabitants of a dying countryside.' Then his bicycle whirrs off, carrying us to the great Rock of Cashel, 'the great mass of buildings in which the whole history of Ireland is concentrated, abandoned by both Churches, exists only on the grudging charity of the Commissioners of Public Works'. It is as though he had taken to heart George Moore's argument that the perfect title for a book about Ireland would be 'Ruin and Weed – ruined castles in a weedy country'. I remember standing with him once, deep underground in the clammy silence of the megalithic passage-grave at Dowth, as he explained, in great high spirits, that Irish civilization began its long, fatal decline in the ninth century.

His novel Dutch Interior (1940) is a bleak study of provincial decay, the decline of intellect, the withering of character into mere personality. It is a savage, tearing and lonely book, a chronicle of spirit wasted and wasting in a provincial backwater. It engages a subject which never, as I recall, appears directly in the stories, yet which obviously loomed large in his life – the position of the artist in a land where enemies of the Spirit are ubiquitous and invisible. It is the only one of his books which Joyce would have liked and approved of. And, significantly, it is the one book lacking in that attribute by which O'Connor set such store – the sound of a man's voice, speaking.

Something of the meaning which that voice held for him, in his stories, is hinted at in the introduction to The Lonely Voice (1962), a series of vivid and intelligent studies of the modern masters of the short story. The introduction, which is contentious and a bit cranky, is not equal to the studies which follow, but has for us here an interest of its own. 'Always in the short story,' he argues, 'there is this sense of outlawed figures wandering about the fringes of society.' We are to see in the short story an attitude of mind that is attracted by 'submerged population groups, whatever these may be at any given time – tramps, lonely idealists, dreamers, and spoiled priests'. The novel can adhere to the classical concept of a civilized society, but 'the short story remains by its very nature remote from the community – romantic, individual-istic, intransigent'.

One pauses over this only for the curious reason that it is his own short fiction which comes first to mind as evidence to the contrary. It speaks from within and with the accents of its community, and, to repeat, it knows to a syllable how everything in that community can be said. Almost any paragraph can suggest this:

> Apart from Farren, Jack's great friends were the Dwyers, a large, loud-mouthed family. The father was a small building contractor, known to his wife as 'poor Dwyer,' whose huffy shyness had never permitted him to get anywhere in life. His wife had ten times his brains and he lectured her as if she were an idiot, and she put up with it as if she were. She was a big, buxom, bonny woman, very devout and very caustic. They had three boys and three girls, and Jack went drinking and bowling with the boys and dancing with the girls until the latter held a council about him and decided, as he was completely incapable of making up his own mind, that they'd better do it for him. It was decided that he should marry Susie, the middle girl. Annie, the youngest, whom he was supposed to favor, was compensated with a blue frock.

Now it is true that the conditions of Jack's future loneliness have been efficiently organized, and an ingenious case for the several lonelinesses of all Dwyers save the brothers might be drawn from the paragraph, but this is scarcely its effect. There is simply too much wicked delight in the knowledge of how they manage affairs at the Dwyer house. But on a re-reading, the scene of community is less strong, for while the voice may like to speak of large families, it is the voice of an only child, of a maid-servant's boy who loved to write of building contractors in their ugly, solid parlors. (Who else would have thought to title a chapter on Chekhov 'The Slave's Son'?)

O'Connor was a fiery, indeed a notorious opponent of the Church temporal, and yet no other Irish writer has written with such persuasive warmth of the community of priests. He could mock with devastating skill those who sentimentalized 'the ould customs', but in 'The Long Road to Ummera' he made a moving small saga of an old peasant woman's loyalty to her past. He dealt professional patriots merciless blows, in his fiction and out of it, but he remained loyal to his lost legion of a rebel community, to

Michael Collins on his last, fatal journey into the hills of Cork, and to Erskine Childers on his fatal journey down from them. It is the communities from which he was separated that he celebrates in that easy voice of a man, talking, and the separation gives to the voice the power which lies just beneath the ease. It is a voice of a man alienated, as Joyce was, from those of whom he wrote. But O'Connor, unlike Joyce, loved those from whom he was alienated, and communities grew in art from that love.

When he was buried, at Dean's Grange, one of the loveliest of his translations from Irish was read beside the grave. It begins:

> *What shall we do for timber?*
> *The last of the woods is down.*
> *Kilcash and the house of its glory*
> *And the bell of the house are gone. . . .*

The note is properly elegiac. But O'Connor himself saw fit to criticize 'Cast a cold eye' as a woefully inappropriate and perverse epitaph for Yeats. And with that as precedent, I shall remember him with a different one.

It is winter's evening in Dublin, when darkness comes with arctic swiftness. The door of Mooney's in Baggot Street bursts open, and Michael comes in, evening paper held in a furious fist, mane of white hair flying. 'Have you heard what they are after doing now in this bloody country?' What they were after doing would then be rehearsed in all its Borgian intricacy, the paper soon being discarded, as an imperfect prompt book. But 'they' must henceforth pursue their plans with circumspection, for at last he can see to it that they don't get away with it.

Oration at Graveside

BRENDAN KENNELLY

Dean's Grange, 12 March 1966

> *Cad a déanfaimid feasta gan admad*
> *Tá deiread na gcoillte ar lár,*
> *Níl tráct ar Cill Cais ná a teaglac*
> *Ní cluinfear a cling go brác –*
> *An áit úd ina gcónáiod an deag bean*
> *Fuair gradam is meidir tar mná;*
> *Bíód íarlai ag tarraing tar toinn ann*
> *Is an tAifreann binn dá rá.*

Michael O'Donovan's translation of that Irish poem, 'Cill Chais', goes like this:

> *What shall we do for timber?*
> *   The last of the woods is down.*
> *Kilcash and the house of its glory*
> *   And the bell of the house are gone,*
> *The spot where that lady waited*
> *   Who shamed all women for grace*
> *When earls came sailing to greet her*
> *   And Mass was said in the place.*

Something of the loss that Ireland and Irish literature have suffered is expressed in these lines, because since the death of Yeats, it can be said of Michael O'Donovan alone that he was not simply a great writer or a lovable man, or an ardent scholar, but an inspiration to all those who knew him.

He was particularly an inspiration to young people. His readiness to help the young was wonderful to see; he would listen to, or read, what the most awkward beginner had to offer; he would suggest criticisms with kindliness and tact; he would go to immense trouble to study a poem or a short story, and then spend considerable time advising the young writer about possible alterations and improvements.

When Michael was around, the air was alive with possibilities. His very presence held a promise of wonderful things. To me, he looked like a king, felt like a poet, spoke like a god. Negative things formed no part of his life or outlook; his emphasis was always on the positive and the possible, especially in his relationship with the young. That is what I meant when I said that he was an inspiration.

In literature he liked to talk and to write about what he called 'The Backward Look', that is Ireland's search for a national identity in the rich sources of myth and saga. I do not claim to speak for my generation, but it is fair to say that Michael O'Donovan's life might be called 'The Forward Look' into a future where young Irishmen and women would know precisely, and with love, what the term 'Irish Heritage' means.

For Michael it meant the attempt to understand life as we at present experience it, by studying the past in all its richness and diversity – its music, art, architecture, literature, history – the entire complex that has produced the Ireland we know, the people we know.

That was his dream and, in following it, he explored and translated ancient Irish poetry, was passionately interested in history and architecture, and sought to integrate all these different threads in a scheme of study which would enable young Ireland to discover the past, know the present and challenge the future.

He was first and foremost a man of vision, an essentially integrating vision, a vision that wanted unity instead of fragmentation.

He fought for this unified vision right up to his last breath, denouncing what seemed to him to disrupt that vision: the censors because a lot of censorship is a frantic rejection of life; the destroyers of beautiful houses because they were annihilating one of the first expressions of an age; and those who neglect our monuments because such neglect is ignorance of a vital aspect of the past.

Conversely, he always praised whatever fortified his vision of unity; intellectual freedom, the ability to speak and write both in Irish and English, the study of Gaelic and Anglo-Irish literature. He wanted to build a bridge between traditions, to show that where many saw division, he could discover unity.

His own life was a connection between generations – he was a living link with Ireland's greatest poet, Yeats. When he spoke of Yeats's death, he chose the following lines as an epitaph. I can do no better than repeat them – because what was true of Yeats was true of Michael O'Donovan; he was a man of greatness and generosity, a man who loved laughter, who escaped bitterness although meeting with disappointments; a passionate man who made himself vulnerable in order that he might inspire.

> *And I choose the laughing lip*
> *That shall not turn from laughing whatever rise or fall;*
> *The heart that grows no bitterer although betrayed by all;*
> *The hand that loves to scatter;*
> *The life like a gambler's throw.*

I hope that that life has found the happy immortality that it deserves.

Towards a Bibliography of Frank O'Connor's Writing

Frank O'Connor was, above all, a short story writer. This was the field of literature in which W. B. Yeats felt he excelled when he compared his impact with that of Anton Chekhov. For this reason special emphasis has been placed on Frank O'Connor's short stories. The collections of his short stories appear first in the list of books and an alphabetical list of his stories later in the bibliography.

Yet there are some who might disagree – those in particular who argue that Frank O'Connor's genius is best expressed in his translations of Old, Middle and Modern Irish poetry, superb translations which often appear, were it possible, to improve on the originals. This was genius involving an insight into the Irish mind through the centuries, and it gave rise to a major scholarly question for the author. As heir to a tradition involving two languages, Irish and English, he thought he could discern a slender thread of cultural unity in the literature of Ireland. This raised a problem which vexed him from his early days, when, during the Civil War for instance, he asked the question in the poem 'On Moyrus' – which of the two languages should he write in? The theme occurs not only in the early poems, but also in his earliest articles. Separate sections are therefore made in the bibliography for his early poems, both originals and translations, and for his early articles. These also involve themes which eventually formed the subject of his books on literary criticism and history.

Frank O'Connor first wrote under his own name, Michael O'Donovan. At an early stage he began to use the pseudonym Frank O'Connor (cf second volume of his autobiography, *My Father's Son*, ch. 5). In one issue of the *Irish Tribune* he wrote a book review over the name Michael O'Donovan and sent a letter to the editor over the pseudonym

Frank O'Connor. This was 25 June 1926. Thereafter he consistently used the pseudonym, but unexpectedly the name Michael O'Donovan appears under an article in the *Bookman* in August 1934.

BOOKS

The books are numbered (E = English, D = Danish, G = German) to facilitate references to his collections of short stories in the alphabetical list of stories which concludes the bibliography.

BOOKS IN ENGLISH

Short story collections

E1 *Guests of the Nation* (Macmillan, London 1931, 1933 : New York 1931).

E2 *Bones of Contention* (Macmillan, New York 1936 : London 1938).

E3 *Three Tales* (limited edition, Cuala Press, Dublin 1941).

E4 *Crab Apple Jelly* (Macmillan, London 1944 : Knopf, New York 1944).

E5 *Selected Stories* (Hour-glass Library series, Fridberg, Dublin 1946).

E6 *The Common Chord* (Macmillan, London 1947 : Knopf, New York 1948).

E7 *Traveller's Samples* (Macmillan, London 1951 : Knopf, New York 1951).

E8 *The Stories of Frank O'Connor* (Knopf, New York 1952 : Hamish Hamilton, London 1953).

E9 *More Stories by Frank O'Connor* (Knopf, New York 1954, 1967).

E10 *Stories by Frank O'Connor* (Vintage, New York 1956).

E11 *Domestic Relations* (Hamish Hamilton, London 1957 : Knopf, New York 1957).

E12 *My Oedipus Complex and Other Stories* (Penguin Books, 1963).

E13 *Collection Two* (Macmillan, London 1964).

E14 *My Oedipus Complex and Other Stories*. English texts with Japanese notes, ed. K. Yamaguchi and A. Sugie (Kōbunsha, Tokyo 1963).

M

E15 *Collection Three* (Macmillan, London 1969).

E15A *A Set of Variations* (Knopf, New York 1969).

E16 *Irish Short Stories*, I, Englische und Amerikanische Leselogen Nr. 39 (Velhagen & Klasing, Bielefeld, Berlin, Hanover).

E17 *Irish Short Stories*, II (as in E16) Nr. 40.

E18 *Irish Short Stories*, ed. Wilhelm Brockhaus (Ferdinand Schöningh, Paderborn).

Anthologies

E19 *Modern Irish Short Stories*, selected with an Introduction by Frank O'Connor (World's Classics no. 560, Oxford University Press, London 1957).

E20 *A Book of Ireland*, edited with an Introduction by Frank O'Connor (Collins National Anthologies, London, Glasgow 1959).

Autobiography

E21 *An Only Child* (Knopf, New York 1961: Macmillan, London 1962, 1965, Papermac 1965).

E22 *My Father's Son* (Macmillan, London 1968: Knopf, New York 1969).

Biography

E23 *The Big Fellow. A Life of Michael Collins* (Nelson, London 1937). Revised edition (Clonmore & Reynolds, Dublin, Burns, Oates, London 1965). See below, *Death in Dublin*.

E23A *Death in Dublin: Michael Collins and the Irish Revolution* [= *The Big Fellow*] (Doubleday, Doran, New York 1937: Templegate, Illinois 1966).

Historical and topographical

E24 *A Picture Book, illustrated by Elisabeth Rivers* (limited edition, Cuala Press, Dublin 1943).

E25 *Irish Miles* (Macmillan, London 1947).

E26 *Leinster, Munster, and Connaught* (The County Books, Robert Hale, London 1950).

Introductions by Frank O'Connor

E27 *Dead Souls*, by Nikolai Gogol (Mentor, New American Library, New York 1961).

E28 *Irish Street Ballads*, by C. O Lochlainn (Corinth Books, New York 1960).

E29 *A Portrait of the Artist as a Young Man*, by James Joyce (Time Reading Program, New York 1964).

E30 *The Tailor and Ansty*, by Eric Cross (Chapman & Hall, London 1964).

Literary criticism and history

E32 *Towards an Appreciation of Literature* (Metropolitan Publishing Co., Dublin 1945).

E32 *The Road to Stratford* (Methuen, London 1948). See below, *Shakespeare's Progress.*

E33 *The Mirror in the Roadway: A Study of the Modern Novel* (Knopf, New York 1956: Hamish Hamilton, London 1957).

E34 *Shakespeare's Progress*, a revised and enlarged edition of *The Road to Stratford* (World Publishing Co., Cleveland, Ohio 1960: Collier Books, New York 1961).

E35 *The Lonely Voice: A Study of the Short Story* (World Publishing Co., Cleveland, Ohio 1962: Nelson, Foster & Scott, Toronto 1963: Meridian Books 1965: Macmillan, London 1963, Papermac 1965: revised and enlarged edition, Bantam, New York 1968).

E36 *The Backward Look: A Survey of Irish Literature* (Macmillan, London/Melbourne/Toronto 1967). See *A Short History of Irish Literature.*

E36A *A Short History of Irish Literature: A Backward Look* [= *The Backward Look*] (G. P. Putnam's Sons, New York 1967).

Novels

E37 *The Saint and Mary Kate* (Macmillan, London 1932, 1936: New York 1932).

E38 *Dutch Interior* (Macmillan, London 1940: Knopf, New York 1940).

M 2

Poetry

E39   *Three Old Brothers and Other Poems* (Centaur Poets, Nelson, London/New York 1936).

Poetry translations from the Irish

E40   *The Wild Bird's Nest: Poems from the Irish by Frank O'Connor with an essay on the character in Irish literature by A.E.* (limited edition, Cuala Press, Dublin 1932).

E41   *The Fountain of Magic* (Macmillan, London 1939).

E42   *Lords and Commons* (limited edition, Cuala Press, Dublin 1938).

E43   *Lament for Art O'Leary*, with illustrations by Jack B. Yeats (limited edition, Cuala Press, Dublin 1940).

E44   *The Midnight Court.* A Rhythmical Bacchanalia from the Irish of Bryan Merriman, with Preface (Fridberg, London/Dublin 1945).

E45   *Kings, Lords, & Commons* (Knopf, New York 1959: Macmillan, London 1961).

E46   *The Little Monasteries* (limited edition, Dolmen Press, Dublin 1963).

E47   *A Golden Treasury of Irish Poetry, A.D. 600–1200.* Irish texts and prose translations. Edited and translated with Introduction by Frank O'Connor and David Greene (Macmillan, London/Melbourne/Toronto 1967).

Theatre

E48   *The Art of the Theatre* (Fridberg, London/Dublin 1947).

TRANSLATIONS INTO GERMAN

Short stories of Frank O'Connor

G1 *Er hat die Hosen an*, trans. Elisabeth Schnack (Nymphenburger Verlagshandlung, Munich 1957).

G2 *Die lange Strasse nach Ummera: Elf Meistererzählungen aus Irland*, trans. Elisabeth Schnack (Diogenes Verlag, Zürich 1959).

G3 *Und freitags Fisch: Sieben Geschichten von irischen Liebes- und Ehepaaren*, trans. Elisabeth Schnack (Diogenes Verlag, Zürich 1958: Taschenbuch 1963).

G4 *Geschichten von Frank O'Connor*, trans. Elisabeth Schnack (Diogenes Verlag, Zürich 1967).

G5 *Bitterer Whisky: Fünf irische Erzählungen*, trans. Elisabeth Schnack, Insel-Bücherei Nr. 732 (Insel-Verlag, Frankfurt a. M. 1912).

G6 *Der Trunkenbold: irische Geschichten*, trans. Elisabeth Schnack (Philipp Reclam Jun., Stuttgart 1963).

Short stories: general anthologies

G7 *Irische Meister der Erzählung*, selected and trans. Elisabeth Schnack (Walter Dorn Verlag, Bremen-Horn 1955).

G8 *Grüne Insel: Erzählungen aus Irland von James Joyce bis James Plunkett*, selected and trans. Elisabeth Schnack (Diogenes Verlag, Zürich 1961).

G9 *Irische Erzähler der Gegenwart: Eine Anthologie*, edited and introduced Elisabeth Schnack (Philipp Reclam Jun., Stuttgart 1965).

Novel

G10 *Die Reise nach Dublin* (= *The Saint and Mary Kate*), trans. Elisabeth Schnack (Diogenes Verlag, Zürich 1961; Taschenbuch 1964; Büchergilde 1965).

Autobiography

G11 *Einziges Kind* (= *An Only Child*), trans. Elisabeth Schnack (Diogenes Verlag, Zürich 1964).

TRANSLATIONS INTO DANISH

Short stories of Frank O'Connor

D1 *Den hellige Dør*, pa Dansk ved Harold Engberg (Gyldendal, København 1954).

THEATRE

Dramatisations of novels and short stories

In the Train, in collaboration with Hugh Hunt, produced Abbey Theatre, 31 May 1937. Text in *The Genius of the Irish Theatre* ed., S. Barnet, M. Berman and W. Burto (Mentor, New American Library, New York 1960) 245.

When I was a Child, adaptation for the stage of 'The Genius' and produced in New York, December 1950.

Guests of the Nation, adapted by Neil McKenzie and produced New York, 1957. Text in *Dramatists Play Service, 1960.*

Three Hand Reel, adaptation by Paul Mayer of the three stories, 'Bridal Night', 'Eternal Triangle' and 'The Frying Pan'. Produced in New York, December 1966.

The Saint and Mary Kate, adapted by Mary Manning, produced Abbey Theatre, March 1968.

Plays written for the theatre

The Invincibles, in collaboration with Hugh Hunt, produced Abbey Theatre in October 1937 and October 1967.

Moses' Rock, in collaboration with Hugh Hunt, produced Abbey Theatre in February 1938.

Time's Pocket, produced at Abbey Theatre in December 1938.

The Statue's Daughter, produced by the Dublin Drama League in December 1941.

TELEVISION

Dramatisations of short stories

The Martyr, adaptation of the short story produced by G. E. Theatre in New York, 1954.

Larry, adaptation of the short story 'My Oedipus Complex', by Geraldine Fitzgerald.

Orphans, adaptation of the short story produced by G. E. Theatre in New York, 1956.

Silent Song, adaptation of the short story, 'Song without Words', by Hugh Leonard and produced by B.B.C. T.V., 2 February 1966. Italia Prize 1967.

Guests of the Nation, a reading by the author on Radio-Telefís Eireann T.V., 1964.

Documentaries

Monitor – filmed interview in Cork (autobiographical), B.B.C. T.V., 19 November 1961 and 12 August 1963.

Horseman Pass By (W. B. Yeats), B.B.C. T.V., 23 January 1966. See also 'A Gambler's Throw', *The Listener*, 17 February 1966.

Self-Portrait (autobiographical), Radio-Telefís Eireann T.V. 2 and 9 January 1962.

An Nodlaig ig Corcaigh (autobiographical) Radio-Telefís Eireann T.V., 24 December 1967.

RADIO

The first radio broadcast that has been traced was made on Radio Eireann, the Irish Broadcasting Station, on 3 January 1937. This was a talk reviewing several books. In the following list of selected broadcasts a number of Frank O'Connor's minor broadcasts, both on Radio Eireann and B.B.C., have been omitted.

Dramatisations of short stories

Country People, adaptation of the short stories 'In the Train', 'The Luceys' and 'The Long Road to Ummera', produced on Radio Eireann, 9 December 1959.

Fighting Men, adaptation of the Short Stories 'Guests of the Nation', 'The Martyr' and 'Private Property', produced by Radio Eireann, 1 February 1959.

Portraits and talks – a selection

'Literary Portraits: Yeats and AE', Radio Eireann, 1939–40.

'Davitt – a Portrait', Radio Eireann, 1940.

'Across St George's channel' (talk), B.B.C. Radio, 27 December 1940. See *The Listener*, January 1941.

'Readings from F. R. Higgins', B.B.C. Radio, 1 March 1941, 26 February 1964.

'An Bóthar go hEanach Dún', Radio Eireann, 16 September 1941.

'Plays and Poetry of W. B. Yeats', B.B.C. Radio, 19 April 1941.

'James Joyce', B.B.C. Radio, 18 May 1944. See *The Listener*, 1 June 1944.

'W. B. Yeats: Reminiscence by a friend', B.B.C. Radio, 4 May 1947. See *The Listener*, May 1947.

'The Art of the Theatre', B.B.C. Radio, 5 March 1948.

'John Bull and His Own Island', B.B.C. Radio, 25 April 1948.

'The Cú Chulainn Sagas', B.B.C. Radio, 24 September 1948, 1 October 1948.

'The Riddle of Swift', B.B.C. Radio, 2 October 1948.

'A. E. Coppard', B.B.C. Radio, 27 November 1948.

'Irish Writers', B.B.C. Radio, 2 December 1948.

'Yeats and the Theatre', B.B.C. Radio, 6 June 1949.

'W. B. Yeats – a Dublin Portrait', B.B.C. Radio, 5 June 1949.

'Portrait of James Joyce', B.B.C. Radio, 13 February 1950.

'My Art and Craft – the Short Story', B.B.C. Radio, 19 October 1951.

'George Moore', B.B.C. Radio, 24 February 1952.

'Architect of His Own Reputation – Anthony Trollope', B.B.C. Radio, 24 July 1954.

'George Bernard Shaw – an Irish Portrait', B.B.C. Radio, 20 September 1954.

'One Man's Way – the Short Story', B.B.C. Radio, 24 June 1959. See also *The Listener*, 23 July 1959.

'Leabhar a theastuigh uaim', Radio Eireann, November 1959.

'An Nodlaig i gCorcaigh', Radio Eireann, December 1959.

'Nodlaig as Baile', Radio Eireann, December 1960.

'Scrapbook for 1921 – Irish Civil War', B.B.C. Radio, 2 October 1961, 17 April 1962.

'Adventures in Translation', B.B.C. Radio, 17 January 1962.

'Interior Voices' (autobiographical), B.B.C. Radio, 13 January 1963.

'The Art of the Short Story', Radio Eireann, 26 January 1964.

'AE – George Russell', B.B.C. Radio, 20 January 1965.

'W. B. Yeats', B.B.C. Radio, 11 and 13 June 1965.

'The Yeats We Knew', Radio Eireann, 21 February 1965.

'Leabharlanna agus mé féin' (autobiographical), Radio Eireann, 11 March 1968.

DISK AND TAPE RECORDINGS

The Irish Tradition, Folkways Record 9825.
James Joyce, Folkways Record 9834.
My Oedipus Complex & The Drunkard, Caedmon Records, TC 1036.
Ireland's Monuments, Tapes – A.C.T., Dublin.
Leabharlanna agus mé féin, Tapes – A.C.T., Dublin.
Oiche Shamhraidh, Tapes – A.C.T., Dublin.
Leabhar a theastuigh uaim, Tapes – A.C.T., Dublin.
An Nodlaig i gCorcaigh, Tapes – A.C.T., Dublin.
Nodlaig as Baile, Tapes – A.C.T., Dublin.

FILMS

Omitted from this section are those books and stories for which film options have recently been acquired, but which had not appeared on the television or cinema screen before June 1968.

Guests of the Nation, adaptation for the movies by amateur group, 1933. Irish Film Society archives.
The Rising of the Moon, adaptation for the movies of the short story 'The Majesty of the Law', produced by Four Provinces Films in 1957.

POETRY

Frank O'Connor's first published piece of writing was an unsigned contribution in the boy's magazine, *Our Boys*. This has not been traced. Three poems were published in *An Long* in 1922 (only 3 issues of *An Long* appeared).

Early poems

'The Rosary', by Michael O'Donovan, in *Catholic Bulletin*, March 1923.
'Suibhne Geilt Speaks', in *Irish Statesman*, 14 March 1925.
'Brightness of Brightness' (trans.), in *Irish Statesman*, 13 June 1925.
'Sever me not from Thy Sweetness' (trans.), in *Irish Statesman*, 21 November 1925.
'Alone in the big town she dreams', in *Irish Statesman*, 9 January 1926.

'Celibacy' (trans.), 'Father Geoffrey Keating sang this', in *Irish Statesman*, 6 February 1926.

'Love', in *Irish Statesman*, 24 April 1926.

'Two Impressions', in *Irish Statesman*, 21 August 1926.

'Return in Harvest', in *Irish Statesman*, 20 November 1926.

'Lullaby of Adventurous Love' (trans.), in *Irish Tribune*, 3 December 1926.

'The Madman' (trans.), in *Irish Statesman*, 1 January 1927.

'On Moyrus', in *Irish Statesman*, 5 February 1927.

'Three Old Brothers', in *Irish Statesman*, 14 May 1927.

'Quest of Dead O'Donovans', in *Irish Statesman*, 20 August 1927.

'An Old Song Re-Written', in *Irish Statesman*, 1 October 1927.

'In Winter', in *Irish Statesman*, 14 January 1928.

'Storm', in *Irish Statesman*, 18 February 1928.

'From Gugan of the Saints', in *Irish Statesman*, 21 April 1928.

'The Home-coming of Dinny Pa', in *Irish Statesman*, 9 June 1928.

'The Hawk', in *Irish Statesman*, 18 August 1928.

'The End of Egan O'Rahilly', in *Irish Statesman*, 13 October 1928.

'Reverie at Dawn' (trans.), in *Irish Statesman*, 30 March 1929.

'Beggars', in *Irish Statesman*, 13 July 1929.

'Prelude', in *Irish Statesman*, 25 January 1930.

'The Stars are Astand', in *Irish Statesman*, 5 April 1930.

'Prayer at Dawn' (trans.), in *Dublin Magazine*, April–June 1932.

'A Learned Mistress' (trans.), *Commonweal*, December 1932.

Early poems in manuscript

'*An Chros*' (1921).

'Ambush' (October 1922).

'My Last Duchess' (1922–3).

'Night in the Cottage' (1922–3).

'Duet' (1922–3).

'On Guard' (1922).

'For the End' (Gormanstown Internment Camp 1923).

'Theocritus on Sunday' (1923–4).

'Philosophy' (1924).

'Priest' (1925); not the translation printed in *The Mentor Book of Irish Poetry* ed. Devin A. Garrity (New York 1965) 293.

'Life'.

'Sonnet'.

'An Old Woman Leaves the Workhouse'.

'On a House Shaken by the Land Agitation' ('With apologies to W. B. Yeats').

'Of Lus na Gaoithe's fall from Grace'.

ARTICLES

During World War II most of Frank O'Connor's sources of revenue as a writer were cut off, and there were times when he doubted the wisdom of his decision to abandon the secure income of a permanent job to dedicate his life to writing. These too were the years when the Irish government couldn't make up its mind whether Frank O'Connor was a Nazi, a Communist or a spy for the imperialist Allies: all Frank O'Connor was doing was cycling around Ireland examining the ruins of our monastic heritage and collecting the topographical evidence for his work on the Irish literary tradition. He was often trailed by baffled detectives as he poked among the weeds of our ancient monuments. It was at this time that a friend, the Editor of the Dublin newspaper the *Sunday Independent*, came to his aid and published a series of his articles and comments. But such was the atmosphere at the time that even the pseudonym Frank O'Connor was unacceptable and so was born the new correspondent Ben Mayo. These current affairs articles are listed under a separate title.

The articles listed include all Frank O'Connor's better-known essays and prose pieces, from the unpopular but brilliantly balanced assessment of James Joyce and the uncompromising interpretation of the Great Famine of 1844–6 in the review of Cecil Woodham-Smith's *The Great Hunger*, to the famous essays, on the short story – 'It's a Lonely Personal Art', and on Irish drama – 'A Lyric Voice in the Irish Theatre' (which have been translated into half a dozen languages), and the accurate if humiliating article 'Ireland' in *Holiday*, 1949. Many of the articles were occasioned by reviewing books, but only a fraction of his book reviews are included in this list.

The articles 'The Art of the Theatre' were lectures given in the town hall of Grimsby as Ferens Lecturer in Fine Arts at the University of Hull.

Autobiographical reminiscences

'A Boy in Prison', in *Life and Letters*, August 1934.
'Child, I know you're going to miss me', in *New Yorker*, 6 December 1958.
'I know where I'm going', in *New Yorker*, 14 February 1959.
'The one day of the year', in *New Yorker*, 19 December 1959.
'An Nodlaigh i gCorcaigh', in *Comhar*, February 1960.
'Go where glory waits thee', in *New Yorker*, 26 March 1960.
'The Hunger Strike', in *Reporter Magazine*, 19 January 1961.
'Rifles, Poems and Curfews', in *Kenyon Review*, Winter 1961.
'Nodlaig as Baile', in *Comhar*, December 1962.
'My Father's Wife', in *Saturday Evening Post*, 26 February 1966.

Early articles

'Mozart', in *An Long*, vol. 1, 1922.
'Solus', in *An Long*, vol. 1, 1922.
'Literature and Life: The poet as professional' in *Irish Statesman*, 3 October 1925.
'Literature and Life: Egan O'Rahilly', in *Irish Statesman*, 30 January 1926.
'Literature and Life: To Spain and the World's Side', in *Irish Statesman*, 2 January 1926.
'Literature and Life: Irish Love Poetry', in *Irish Statesman*, 15 May 1926.
'Literature and Life: An Irish Anthology', in *Irish Statesman*, 12 June 1926.
'The Heart has reasons', in *Irish Tribune*, 25 June 1926.
'Have we a literature', in *Irish Tribune*, 13 August 1926.
'Literature and Life: Classic Verse', in *Irish Statesman*, 23 July 1927.
'Munster Fine Arts Exhibition', in *Irish Statesman*, 19 November 1927.
'The Traveller in the Mask', in *Irish Statesman*, 22 September 1928.
'Literature and Life: Heine', in *Irish Statesman*, 23 March 1929.
'Literature and Life: the evocation of the past – Proust', in *Irish Statesman*, 1 June 1929.
'Gaelic Drama: at the Peacock', in *Irish Statesman*, 18 January 1930.
'Abbey-cum-Boccaccio', in *Irish Statesman*, 22 February 1930.
'Joyce – The Third Period', in *Irish Statesman*, 12 April 1930.

Gaelic literature

'Two Languages', by Michael O'Donovan, in *Bookman*, August 1934.
'The Gaelic Tradition in Literature', in *Ireland Today*, nos. 1 and 2,
June–July 1936.
'The Future of Irish Literature', in *Horizon*, February 1942.
'Irish Literature', in *Anglo-Irish Literature*, ed. W. R. Rodgers (Oxford
1968).

General

'To any would-be writer', in *The Bell*, March 1941.
'At the Microphone', in *The Bell*, March 1942.
'The art of architecture', in *Sunday Independent*, 6 January 1946.
'Ireland is a paradise for prigs', in *Sunday Independent*, 7 July 1946.
'Is this a dagger' (satire), in *Nation Magazine*, 26 April 1958.
'Censorship', in *The Dubliner*, no. 2, March 1962.
'Understanding your dreams', in *Vogue*, November 1967.

History

'The Accusing Ghost of Roger Casement', in *New York Times Book
Review*, 17 November 1957.
'The Ghost of Roger Casement', in *Irish Times*, 6 June 1964.
'Patrick the Ulsterman', in *Irish Times*, 17 May 1962.
'Murder Unlimited' (The Great Famine in Ireland), in *Irish Times*,
10 October 1962.
'A Man of Iron' (Arthur Griffith), in *New York Times Book Review*,
30 March 1960.
'For a 200th Birthday' (Mozart), in *Harper's Bazaar*, January 1956.
'John Bull's Other History', in *New York Times Book Review*, 19 March
1961.

Literary criticism, essays and history

'James Joyce – a Postmortem', in *The Bell*, 5 February 1942.
'Shakespeare of the Drawing Room' (Jane Austen), in *Irish Times*,
11 August 1945.

'Stendhal', in *Irish Times*, 25 August 1945.

'Charles Dickens', in *Irish Times*, 8 September 1945.

'Flaubert', in *Irish Times*, 22 September 1945.

'Trollope', in *Irish Times*, 6 October 1945.

'The Extraordinary Story of Jonathan Swift', in *Sunday Independent*, 21 October 1945.

'Tolstoy and Turgenev', in *Irish Times*, 27 October 1945.

'Thomas Hardy', in *Irish Times*, 10 November 1945.

'Anton Chekhov', in *Irish Times*, 24 November 1945.

'Somerville and Ross', in *Irish Times*, 15 December 1945.

'The Novel Approach' (novelists' conference at Harvard), in *New York Times Book Review*, 23 August 1953.

'And it's a lonely personal art', in *New York Times Book Review* 12 April 1953, and *Highlights of Modern Literature* (Mentor, New American Library, New York 1954).

'A matter-of-fact problem in the writing of the Novel', in *New York Times Book Review*, 12 December 1954.

'The last of the liberals' (Chekhov), in *New York Times Book Review*, 24 April 1955.

'Jane Austen and the flight from fancy', in *Yale Review*, September 1955.

'Die Kurzgeschichte', in *Irische Meister der Erzählung* G7 (Dorn, Bremen-Horn 1955).

'A good Short Story must be news' (Liam O'Flaherty), in *New York Times Book Review*, 10 June 1956.

'The Novelist as Politician', in *New York Times Book Review*, 31 March 1957.

'Joyce and his brother', in *Nation*, 1 February 1958.

'Shadows on the Artist's Portrait', in *New York Times Book Review*, 24 August 1958.

'A Writer who refused to pretend' (Chekhov), in *New York Times Book Review*, 17 January 1960, and *Opinions and Perspectives*, ed. F. Brown (Houghton Mifflin, Boston 1964) 126.

'From Jane Austen to Joseph Conrad', in *Victorian Studies*, March 1960.

'The Modesty of Literature', in *New York Times Book Review*, 15 January 1961.

'Tell Dublin I miss her', in *New York Times Book Review*, 25 March 1962.

'Country Matters' (Maupassant), in *Kenyon Review*, Autumn 1962.

'The Girl at the Gaol Gate' (Mary Lavin), in *Kenyon Review*, Spring 1963.

'The Slave's Son' (Chekhov), in *Kenyon Review*, Winter 1963.

'A Master's Mixture' (Chekhov), in *New York Times Book Review*, 1 March 1964.

'The Buck' (Gogarty), in *Spectator*, 26 June 1964.

'Awkward but alive' (Patrick Kavanagh), in *Spectator*, 31 July 1964.

'But what of the author?' (Gogol), in *New York Times Book Review*, 6 September 1964.

'The Small Genius' (James Stephens), in *Spectator*, 7 May 1965.

'All the Olympians' (Synge, Gregory and Yeats), in *Saturday Review*, 10 December 1966.

'Why don't you write about America?', in *Mademoiselle*, April 1967.

'James Joyce – Thesis and Antithesis', in *American Scholar*, Summer 1967.

Literary reminiscences

'Two friends – Yeats and AE', in *Yale Review*, September 1939.

'AE – a portrait', in *The Bell*, November 1940.

'The Old Age of a Poet' (W. B. Yeats), in *The Bell*, February 1941.

'Quarrelling with Yeats', in *Esquire*, December 1964.

'Willie is so silly' (W. B. Yeats), in *Vogue*, March 1965.

'The Scholar' (Osborn Bergin), in *Kenyon Review*, Spring 1965.

'W. B. Yeats', in *The Critic*, December 1966–January 1967.

'Bring in the Whiskey now Mary' (AE), in *New Yorker*, 12 August 1967.

Poetry

'The Midnight Court', in *The Bell*, May 1941.

'Personal Anthologies', in *The Bell*, December 1943.

'Prospectus for an anthology', in *Nation*, 10 November 1956.

'The Nun of Beare', in *Kilkenny Magazine*, Spring 1962.

Theatre and drama

'Synge', in *The Irish Theatre* ed. Lennox Robinson (Macmillan, London 1939).

'The Art of the Theatre: I. the audience', in *The Bell*, March 1945.

'The Art of the Theatre: II. the writer', in *The Bell*, April 1945.

'The Art of the Theatre: III. the actor', in *The Bell*, May 1945.

'The Art of the Theatre: IV. the actor', in *The Bell*, June 1945.

'A lyric voice in the Irish theatre' (W. B. Yeats), in *New York Times Book Review*, 31 May 1953, and *Highlights of Modern Literature*, and *The Genius of the Irish Theatre* ed. S. Barnet, M. Berman and W. Burto (Mentor, New American Library, New York 1960) 354.

'The Life and Death of a Theatre' (Abbey), in *Theatre Arts Magazine*, 1955.

'Sean O'Casey and the Ghosts', in *Holiday*, January 1956.

'The Most American Playwright' (Arthur Miller), in *Holiday*, February 1956.

'St Joans, from Arc to Lark' (Anouilh, *The Lark*), in *Holiday*, March 1956.

'Comedy and Comediennes', in *Holiday*, May 1956.

'Joyce, Colum, Johnston, Meredith', in *Theatre Arts Magazine*, 1958.

'The Actor', in *Drama Critique*, VI (Winter 1963).

Topographical and travel

'Three Churches', in *The Bell*, May 1942.

'In Galway, Kerry and Clare', in *The Bell*, June 1942.

'In Connemara', in *Irish Times*, 14 August 1943.

'South Tipperary', in *Irish Times*, 11 September 1943.

'Carlow, Poor but Proud', in *Irish Times*, 15 January 1944.

'Kilkenny', in *Irish Times*, 12 February 1944.

'Ireland', in *Holiday*, December 1949.

'In Quest of Beer' (England), in *Holiday*, January 1957.

'A Walk in New York', in *Holiday*, November 1958.

'The Holy Places of Ireland', in *Holiday*, April 1963.

'Regency Colonial' (Cork), in *Spectator*, 11 June 1965.

Tributes

'Homage to Jim Larkin' (poem), in *Irish Times*, 9 December 1944.

'John F. Kennedy', in *A Tribute to John F. Kennedy*, ed. P. Salinger and S. Vanocur (Encyclopaedia Britannica, Chicago 1964) 97.

Frank O'Connor in the Sunday Independent

'The disgrace of our libraries and bookshops', 25 March 1962.

'The neglect of our historical monuments', 20 May 1962.

'This is provincialism' (libraries and art), 29 July 1962

'The Casement Diary mystery', 9 September 1962.

'Plays: the International Theatre Festival, Dublin', 30 September 1962.

'Plays: the International Theatre Festival, Dublin', 7 October 1962.

'Does Kinsella lead the Poets' (review), 14 October 1962.

'That dreadful breed I call the lace curtain Irish', (review) 18 November 1962.

'165 places still remember Lug' (review), 9 December 1962.

'The Childhood of Jesus' (poem – trans.), 23 December 1962.

'All the way from Finn to Finnegan' (review), 3 February 1963.

'The abuse of our heritage: Georgian Dublin and Bunratty', 17 February 1963.

'A Golden Treasury of Irish Verse' (series I, 12 poems), 24 February to 5 May 1963. *See E47 above.*

'St Patrick was an outsider' (review essay), 17 March 1963.

'Are we being fair to Sean O'Casey', 12 May 1963.

'Professor Binchy and the town called Charleville', 21 July 1963.

'The Abbey Theatre, Past and Present', 8 September 1963.

'Two poems by Gerald, Earl of Desmond: "The last raid" A.D. 1381, "The widower's bed" A.D. 1392' (trans.), 22 September 1963.

'Plays: the Dublin Theatre Festival', 29 September 1963.

'Plays: the Dublin Theatre Festival', 6 October 1963.

'Shakespeare' (review), 13 October 1963.

'The Arts Council', 3 November 1963.

'Our Crumbling Heritage – the Restoration of our Monuments' (colour supplement, illustrated), 17 November 1963.

'Tribute to John F. Kennedy', 24 November 1963.

'The Little Man in the Big Rising' (Sean T. O'Kelly's *Memoirs* reviewed), 1 December 1963.

'Our National Monuments – Clonmacnois and Clontooskert' (illustrated), 7 June 1964.

'A neglected monument – Glendalough' (illustrated), 14 June 1964.

'Our greatest monument – our greatest disgrace: Cashel' (illustrated), 21 June 1964.

'Jerpoint Abbey and Kilkenny' (illustrated), 28 June 1964.

'A Masterpiece of Irish Art – Holy Cross Abbey' (illustrated), 5 July 1964.

'Shame on us – Athassel Priory, Ennis Abbey, Dysert O'Dea, Quin Abbey' (illustrated), 12 July 1964.

'Books on Ireland' (review), 20 September 1964.

'New Grange Tombs', 27 September 1964.

'Plays: the Dublin Theatre Festival', 27 September 1964.

'Plays: the Dublin Theatre Festival', 4 October 1964.

'A Golden Treasury of Irish Verse' (series II, 11 poems), 15 November 1964 to 24 January 1965. *See* E47 *above*.

'The book nobody knows' (review essay), 13 December 1964.

'Yeats', 13 June 1965.

'Irish Monuments – mystery man takes over', 19 September 1965.

'For the conversion of Professor Stanford' (literature in Irish), 28 November 1965.

'The case for Roger Casement', 16 January 1966.

'Michael Collins, no plaster saint', 23 January 1966.

'Literature and the lashers' (review), 6 February 1966.

Ben Mayo in the Sunday Independent

'Irish ruins shocked visitors', 28 March 1943.

'Why not homes as well as pensions for Ministers', 11 April 1943.

'Critic waves and nonsense waves', 18 April 1943.

'Pensions for great writers: Finland's plan', 25 April 1943.

'Save our old mansions from the speculators', 9 May 1943.

'Radio Eireann banned "foreign" dance music', 16 May 1943.

'The Clare people need books', 23 May 1943.

'Should we abolish Irish history', 6 June 1943.

'People rot in slums, die of tuberculosis . . . if they know Irish', 13 June 1943.

'What are we doing to win the peace', 4 July 1943.

'Culture in mud cabins and four-hand reels', 11 July 1943.

'Our Irish towns have their attractions', 18 July 1943.

'This talk about Education', 25 July 1943.

'Education systems that produce quarrels', 1 August 1943.

'A grilled steak can overrule prejudices', 8 August 1943.

'People cannot do without a purpose in their lives', 15 August 1943.

'A book industry that is greatly neglected', 22 August 1943.

'Should make us sit up', 29 August 1943.

'Our exiles may influence our future', 5 September 1943.

'The people are fallible, but they must be trusted', 12 September 1943.

'Only sort of government that counts in the long run', 19 September 1943.

'M.O.H.'s are the people's genuine friends', 26 September 1943.

'Fianna Fail's attitude to P.R. system', 3 October 1943.

'Board of control for Irish theatres', 10 October 1943.

'Eire's choice – food or money?', 17 October 1943.

'What kind of tourists do we want?', 24 October 1943.

'Have our politicians grown too old?', 31 October 1943.

'Irish – and how to revive it', 7 November 1943.

'An Irish Legion of Honour', 14 November 1943.

'In fond and loving memory . . .', 21 November 1943.

'Levelling the community down', 28 November 1943.

'Paid £1,000 for being a good citizen', 5 December 1943.

'Getting a toy for Christmas', 12 December 1943.

'Ben Mayo writes to Santa Claus', 19 December 1943.

'That Ireland again be part of Dublin', 26 December 1943.

'Pouring millions down the drain of artificial idleness', 2 January 1944.

'Today Ireland needs another Brian Boru', 16 January 1944.

'Making our countryside fit to live in', 23 January 1944.

'Buildings that show something is wrong', 6 February 1944.

'Art and "Gas"', 20 February 1944.

'History is damned by Henry Ford, but . . .', 27 February 1944.

'One's second thoughts are best', 5 March 1944.

'Agonies of practice recipe for champions', 12 March 1944.

'Before we can resume our march we must . . .', 19 March 1944.

'Turf is bad and dear: why not controlled?', 26 March 1944.

'Education is left at the post', 16 April 1944.

'Let us give a hand to the farmers', 23 April 1944.

'Is a Dublin man more English than a Clareman?', 30 April 1944.

'Partition – the people are bewildered', 7 May 1944.

'The next five years will be fateful or fatal', 14 May 1944.

'In normal countries, with normal politicians . . .', 21 May 1944.

'One of the crucial moments in our history', 28 May 1944.

'Problem in re-education of parents', 4 June 1944.

'The surest way to make a profit is . . .', 11 June 1944.

'Gallery of dreams that did not come true', 18 June 1944.

'A children's freedom war has restored', 2 July 1944.

'The Gael and start of our national movement', 16 July 1944.

'Dublin of future may be menace to Ireland', 23 July 1944.

'Where is planning leading us?', 30 July 1944.

'The Irish empire overseas', 6 August 1944.

'Tests by which Eire falls', 13 August 1944.

'War has helped the growth of vocational organisation', 20 August 1944.

'Planning ahead, but are we forgetting the present?', 27 August 1944.

'Are Irish people lazy?', 3 September 1944.

'Give the citizens a chance', 17 September 1944.

'A dress reform for Irish farmers', 24 September 1944.

'Danger of State control', 1 October 1944.

'Same old hobby-horses go round and round', 15 October 1944.

'Must the Irish railways be abandoned?', 22 October 1944.

'A campaign against foolish talk', 29 October 1944.

'Ireland's place in a turbulent world', 12 November 1944.

'Our farmer's wives are not a race of foreign beauties', 26 November 1944.

'The sense of proportion is important', 3 December 1944.

'Are we serious about abolishing partition?', 10 December 1944.

'Drawing northern Irish youth closer to Great Britain', 17 December 1944.

'And on Earth Peace . . .', 24 December 1944.

'Growth of Dublin and Belfast: a Problem', 31 December 1944.

'High moral standard is essential for deputies', 7 January 1945.

'The newspapers of the future', 21 January 1945.

'Dublin is as "English" today as it was 30 years ago', 28 January 1945.

'Limerick urged to launch out on own', 4 February 1945.

'The urge for security has great dangers', 11 February 1945.

'Don't forget our scientists and inventors', 18 February 1945.

'Information wanted, please', 25 February 1945.

'Will women of France give a world lead?', 4 March 1945.

'Learning from the Ascendancy!', 11 March 1945.

'St Patrick's Day: some reflections', 18 March 1945.

'Dublin's disgrace', 25 March 1945.

'The "export" of doctors, "import" of scientists', 1 April 1945.

'Small nations and the world's future', 6 May 1945.

'Our relations with Great Britain', 13 May 1945.

'Mr de Valera and Mr Churchill', 20 May 1945.

'Bevin – Big man in Britain to-day', 27 May 1945.

'Ireland and the Commonwealth – friendly co-operation or isolation?', 22 July 1945.

'We are in it, states the Taoiseach's paper', 29 July 1945.

'Ruin and loss in Ireland', 23 September 1945.

ALPHABETICAL LIST OF SHORT STORIES

The short stories have been reprinted in a large number of periodicals and anthologies of short stories. Only the more important of these sources are mentioned in this list. The collections referred to are those numbered in the lists of books above.

'Achilles' Heel': *New Yorker*, 1 November 1958; E13, E15A, G5; trans. German 'Die Achillesferse'.

'Act of Charity, An': *New Yorker*, 6 May 1967; E15, E15A.

'Adventure': *Atlantic Monthly*, January 1953.

'Adventuress, The': *Far and Wide*, 22 December 1948.

'After Fourteen Years': *Dublin Magazine*, April 1929; read by author B.B.C. Radio, 14 March 1938; E1; *Best British Short Stories* (1929).

'Alec': E1.

'American Wife, The': *New Yorker*, 25 March 1961; E15, E15A; *Winter's Tales*, 8 (1962).

'Anchors': *Harper's Bazaar*, October 1952; E15, E15A.

'And we in herds thy game' (= 'Star that bids the shepherd fold' = 'The Shepherds', see below).

'Androcles and the Army': *Atlantic Monthly*, May 1958; Radio Eireann, 25 December 1958; E13, E15A, G6; trans. German 'Androklus und die Soldaten', also Flemish.

'Attack': E1.

'Awakening, The': *Dublin Magazine*, July 1928.

'Babes in the Wood, The': *New Yorker*, 8 March 1947; E6, E8, G6; trans. German 'Die Kinder im Wald'.

'Bachelor's Story, A': *New Yorker*, 30 July 1955; *John Bull*, October 1956; E11, G3; trans. German 'Geschichte eines Junggesellen', also Dutch.

'Baptismal' (= 'A Spring Day'): *American Mercury*, March 1951.

'Black Drop, The': *Lovat Dickson's Magazine*.

'Book of Kings, The': read on Radio Eireann, 15 November 1940.

'Bones of Contention': *Yale Review*, June 1932; E2, E5, G2; *Best British Short Stories* (1933); trans. German 'Der Zankapfel'.

'Bridal Night, The': *Harper's Bazaar*, July 1939; *The Bell*, December 1941; *Life Story*, September 1945; *Magpie Magazine*, September 1951; B.B.C. Radio, 3 December 1947 and 23 February 1962; E3,

N

E4, E8, E12, G2, G7, G8; trans. German 'Die Brautnacht', also Danish, Swedish and Flemish.

'Brief for Oedipus' (= 'Counsel for Oedipus'): E9; *The World of Law*, vol. 1, no. 13.

'Case for the Roarer, A' (= 'Legal Aid', *see below*): *Harper's Bazaar*, December 1946; *Argosy*, May 1951.

'Cheapjack, The' (= 'The New Teacher', *see below*): B.B.C. Radio, 19 November 1942; E8, E12.

'Cheat, The': *Saturday Evening Post*, 8 May 1965; *Nova*, December 1965; E15, E15A; *Winter's Tales*, 13 (1967).

'Christmas Morning' (= 'The Thief', *see below*): *New Yorker*, 21 December 1946; read by author B.B.C. Radio, 20 December 1948 and 29 December 1950; B.B.C. T.V., 24 September 1956; E8; trans. German 'Der Weihnachtsmorgen'.

'Climber, The': *Harper's Bazaar*, April 1940; read by author B.B.C. Radio, 12 March 1938; *Best Broadcast Stories* (Faber & Faber 1943).

'Conversion, The': *Harper's Bazaar*, March 1951; *Sunday Independent*, December 1967.

'Corkerys, The': *New Yorker*, 30 April 1966; *Woman's Mirror*, June 1966; E15, E15A; trans. Dutch.

'Cornet Player who betrayed Ireland, The': *Harper's Bazaar*, November 1947; *Irish Writing*, April 1948. *See* 'Solo on Gabriel's Trumpet'.

'Crossroads' (= 'First Love', *see below*): *New Yorker*, 23 February 1952.

'Custom of the Country, The': E6, E9, E10, E13; *English Story*, 6th Series (1945).

'Counsel for Oedipus' (= 'Brief for Oedipus', *see above*): E9.

'*Darcy i dTír na nÓg*' (not a translation of the next story): *Nuascéalaíocht 1940–1950*, ed. Tomas de Bhaldraithe (Dublin 1952).

'Darcy in the Land of Youth': *New Yorker*, 15 January 1949; E7, E9, E13.

'Day at the Seaside, A' (= 'Old Fellows', *see below*): *The Bell*, January 1941.

'Daydreams': *New Yorker*, 23 March 1957; *Lilliput*, May 1958; E11, G3; trans. German 'Der Träumer'.

'Don Juan's Apprentice' (= 'The Sorcerer's Apprentice', *see below*): *Harper's Bazaar*, August 1954.

'Don Juan Retired': E6, E9; *Selected Writing No. 4* (1945).

'Don Juan's Temptation': *Magasinet* (Copenhagen), 24 January 1953; E6, E8, E12, G4; trans. German 'Don Juans Versuchung', Danish 'Don Juans Fristelse', also Italian.

'Drunkard, The': *New Yorker*, 3 July 1948; *Cornhill Magazine*, Autumn 1948; *World Digest*, 1948; *Argosy*, November 1949; read by author B.B.C. Radio, 11 May 1949; B.B.C. T.V., 24 January 1953; E7, E8, E10, G6, D1; *44 Irish Short Stories*; trans. German 'Der Trunkenbold', Danish 'Drukkenbolten', also Flemish.

'Duke's Children, The': *New Yorker*, 16 June 1956; *John Bull*, July 1956; Radio Eireann, 6 June 1959; B.B.C. Radio, 6 October 1965; E11, E12; trans. Danish 'Forbyttede Børn', also Swedish.

'English Soldier, The': *Yale Review*, December 1934; E2.

'Eternal Triangle' (= 'The Rising' = 'The Tram', *see below*): E9, G1; trans. German 'Ein trauriger Held'.

'Expectation of Life': *New Yorker*, 13 August 1955; E11, G4; trans. German 'Die Zukunft vor Augen', also Danish.

'Face of Evil, The': *New Yorker*, 3 April 1954; E9.

'Faith moved his Dictionaries': *Everyman*, 10 May 1935.

'Father and Son': E9, E13, G1; trans. German 'Vater und Sohn'.

'Father Fogarty's Island' (= 'The Mass Island', *see below*): *John Bull*, 29 August 1959.

'First Confession' (= 'Repentance', *see below*): *Lovat Dickson's Magazine*, January 1935; *Harper's Bazaar*, March 1939; read by author B.B.C. Radio, 20 February 1944 (repeats) and B.B.C. T.V., 6 November 1952; E5, E7, E8, E12, G2; *Best British Short Stories* (1940); *Book of Stories*, ed. Guttman and Harkness (New York 1955); trans. German 'Die erste Beichte', also Danish, Italian, Swedish.

'First Love' (= 'Crossroads', *see above*): *New Yorker*, 23 February 1952; E8, E12.

'Fish for Friday': *New Yorker*, 18 June 1955; E11, E13, G3; trans. German 'Und freitags Fisch'.

'Flowering Trees, The': *Ireland To-day*, December 1936; *Harper's Bazaar*, August 1938.

'Francis' (= 'Pity'): *New Yorker*, 13 November 1954.

'Freedom': E8.

'Friends of the Family': *Reginald Moore's Modern Reading*, November 1946; E6.

'Frying Pan, The': E6, E9, E13, G4; *trans.* German 'Bei lebendigem Leibe'.

'Genius, The' (= 'The Sissy', *see below*): E11, E12, G1; *Winter's Tales*, 1 (1955); trans. German 'Das Genie'.

'Grand Vizier's Daughters, The': E3, E4, G6; trans. German 'Die Töchter des Grosswesirs'.

'Grandeur': *Ireland To-day*, August 1936.

'Great Man, A': *New Yorker*, 10 May 1958; E15, E15A.

'Guests of the Nation': *Atlantic Monthly*, January 1931; E1, E5, E9, E10, E13, G2; trans. German 'Eine kleine Grube im Moor', French 'Les hôtes de la nation', *Figaro Littéraire*, 18 August 1968, also Flemish and Slovak.

'Holy Door, The': E6, E8, G3, D1; trans. Danish 'Den helige Dør', German 'Die heilige Tür'.

'House that Johnny Built, The': *The Bell*, March 1944; read by author B.B.C. Radio, 10 February 1943; E4, E8, G2; trans. German 'Johnny baute sich ein Haus'.

'Hughie': *The Bell*, October 1941.

'Idealist, The': *New Yorker*, 18 February 1950; *Irish Writing*, March 1951; read by author B.B.C. Radio, 17 March 1949 and 4 March 1964; E7, E8, E10, D1, G4; trans. Danish 'Idealisten', German 'Der Idealist' and 'Die Woche der Idealist', also Italian.

'Impossible Marriage, The': *Woman's Day*, March 1957; E15, E15A.

'In the Train': *Lovat Dickson's Magazine*, June 1935; B.B.C. Radio, 14 September 1948; E2, E5, E8, E10, E12, G2, G5, G7; trans. German 'In der Bahn'.

'Jerome': read by author B.B.C. Radio, 2 May 1951; E7, E9, G1; trans. German 'Jerome Schädel'.

'Jo' (= 'Soldiers are we', *see below*): E1.

'Judas' (= 'The Rivals' = 'Night of Stars', *see below*): E6, E9, E10, E13, E16, G1; trans. German 'Judas' also French and Italian.

'Jumbo's Wife': E1, E5, G5; trans. German 'Jumbos Frau'.

'Ladies of the House' (= 'Lonely Rock', *see below*): *Harper's Magazine*, October 1954.

'Lady Brenda': *Harper's Bazaar*, December 1958.

'Lady in Dublin' (= 'Lady of the Sagas'): *Today's Woman*, October 1946.

'Lady of the Sagas' (= 'Lady in Dublin'): E7, E9.

'Landlady, The': *Penguin New Writing*, no. 37 (1949).

'Last Post, The': *Irish Times*, 29 November 1941.

'Late Henry Conran, The': E1.

'Laughter': E1.

'Legal Aid' (= 'A case for the Roarer', *see above*): *Harper's Bazaar*, December 1946; *Argosy*, May 1951; E7, E8, E10; trans. Danish.

'Life of Your Own, A': *Saturday Evening Post*, 13 February 1965; E15, E15A.

'Little Mother, The': *Harper's Bazaar*, July 1953; E9, E13.

'Lodgers, The': read by author B.B.C. Radio, 15 September 1938.

'Lofty': E2.

'Lonely Rock' (= 'Ladies of the House', *see above*): E9; trans. German 'Einsamkeit'.

'Long Road to Ummera, The': *The Bell*, October 1940; E4, E8, E10, G2; trans. German 'Die lange Strasse nach Ummera', also Flemish.

'Lost Fatherlands': *New Yorker*, 8 May 1954, E15, E15A.

'Luceys, The': E4, E8, E10.

'Mac's Masterpiece': *London Mercury*, May 1938; *Best British Short Stories* (1939); *Short Stories for Study* (New York 1941, 1950).

'Machine Gun Corps in Action': E1; trans. Danish 'Maskingevaer-skytterne Arbejder'.

'Mad Lomasneys, The' (= 'The Wild Lomasneys', *see below*): E4, E9, E10, E13.

'Majesty of the Law, The': *Fortnightly Review*, August 1935; *Daily Express*, 23 September 1951; read by author B.B.C. Radio, 20 January 1948 and 27 January 1964, and Radio Eireann, 29 January 1956; E2, E5, E8, E10, E12, E14, G2; *44 Irish Short Stories*; trans. French 'La Majesté de la loi', German 'Ja, das Gesetz!', also Swedish.

'Man of the House, The': *New Yorker*, 3 December 1949; read by author B.B.C. Radio, 16 November 1949, 20 November 1950 and 2 January 1966; Radio Eireann, January 1956; N.B.C., November 1955; E7, E9, E13, E16, G1; trans. Danish 'Manden i Huset', German 'Er hat die Hosen an', also Slovak.

'Man of the World, The': *New Yorker*, 28 July 1956; E11, G4; *Stories from the New Yorker 1950–1960*; trans. German 'Ein Mann von Welt'.

'Man that stopped, The': *Bookman*, August 1934; E2.

'Martyr, The': *John Bull Magazine*, 15 December 1951; *Harper's Magazine*, February 1953; E15, E15A.

'Masculine Principle': *New Yorker*, 24 June 1950; *Argosy*, August 1950; E7, E8, E10.

'Masculine Protest': *New Yorker*, 28 June 1952; read by author B.B.C. Radio, 18 June 1954; E9, E15, E16, G1; *Pick of Today's Stories* (Pudney, 1956); trans. German 'Wenn Männer protestieren', also Swedish.

'Mass Island, The' (= 'Father Fogarty's Island', *see above*): *New Yorker*, 10 January 1959; E15, E15A.

'May Night': *Life and Letters*, April 1935.

'Michael's Wife': *Lovat Dickson's Magazine*, February 1935; E2, E5, G2; *Best British Short Stories* (1935), trans. German 'Michaels Frau'.

'Minority, A': *New Yorker*, 28 September 1957; E15, E15A.

'Miracle, The': E6, E9, E13, G1; trans. German 'Das Wunder'.

'Miracle, The' (not same as preceding story): *Life and Letters*, May 1934.

'Miser, The': *Selected Writing*, no. 3 (Winter, 1944); E4, E8, E12: trans. Danish 'Gnieren'.

'Mortal Coil, This': *New American Mercury*, December 1950; E7, E13.

'Mother's Warning, A': *Saturday Evening Post*, 7 October 1967; E15.

'Murderer, The' (= radio version of 'First Confession', *see above*): B.B.C. Radio, 31 March 1948 and 16 February 1966.

'Music When Soft Voices Die': *New Yorker*, 11 January 1958; E15A.

'My Da': *New Yorker*, 25 October 1947; *British Harper's Bazaar*, November 1947; read by author B.B.C. Radio, 23 July 1951; E8; *55 Short Stories from the New Yorker* (1949).

'My First Protestant': E7, E9, E13.

'My Oedipus Complex': *To-day's Woman*, December 1950; *Irish Writing no. 20*, November 1952; *Daily Express*, 21 November 1951; *Parents' Magazine*, February 1965; read by author B.B.C. Radio, 14 November 1950 and 13 October 1963; E8, E10, E12, E14, G3, D1; trans. German 'Mein Ödipus-Komplex', Danish 'Mit Ödipuskompleks', also Dutch, Finnish, Swedish, Italian, Hungarian.

'New Teacher, The' (= 'The Cheapjack', *see above*): E4.

'News for the Church': *New Yorker*, 22 September 1945; E6, E8, E10, G3; trans. German 'Die Sünderin' and 'Eva nach dem Sündenfall', also Danish and French.

'Night of Stars' (= 'Judas', *see above*): *The Bell*, March 1942; B.B.C. Radio, 26 May 1944.

'Nightpiece with Figures': E1.

'Old Age Pensioners': E7; trans. Danish 'Pensionisternes Store Dag'.

'Old Faith, The': E9, E13, G1; trans. German 'Der alte Glaube'.

'Old Fellows' (= 'A Day at the Seaside', *see above*): *The Bell*, January 1941; B.B.C. Radio, 16 April 1943, 24 May 1948; E4, E8, G4; trans. German 'Der Beschüter', also Flemish.

'Orphans': *Mademoiselle*, July 1956; G.E. Theatre T.V., 1956; E11, G4; trans. German 'Verwaist'.

'Orpheus and his Lute': *Esquire*, January 1936; B.B.C. Radio, 30 August 1963, also Radio Eireann; E2, E9, E10; trans. Danish 'Orfeus og hans lyre'.

'Out-and-out Free Gift, An': *New Yorker*, 26 October 1957; E15, E15A.

'Paragon, The': *Esquire*, October 1957; E11, E12, G4; trans. German 'Der Wunderknabe'.

'Pariah, The': *New Yorker*, 8 September 1956; E11.

'Party, The': *New Yorker*, 14 December 1957; Radio Eireann, 1 January 1959; E15, E15A.

'Patriarch, The': E1.

'Peasants': *An Long*, vol. 1, 1922; *Lovat Dickson's Magazine*; B.B.C. Radio, 28 February 1947 and 27 January 1949; E2, E5, E8, E18, G2, G7; trans. Danish 'Bønder', German 'Bauern'.

'Peddler, The': *Irish Tribune*, 26 November 1926.

'Picture, The': *Irish Statesman*, 6 April 1929.

'Pity' (= 'Francis', *see above*): E11, E12; trans. German 'Mitleid'.

'Pretender, The': *New Yorker*, 2 December 1950; *The Bell*, Autumn 1953; E8, E10; trans. Flemish.

'Private Property': *Evening News*, June 1950; E11, E13.

'Procession of Life': E1, E13, G4; trans. German 'So ist das Leben'.

'Public Opinion': *Mademoiselle*, September 1957; B.B.C. Radio, 1 January 1959; E15, E15A.

'Rainy Day, A': *John O'London's Weekly*, August 1938.

'Repentance' (= 'First Confession', *see above*): *Lovat Dickson's Magazine*, January 1935.

'Requiem': *New Yorker*, 29 June 1957; read by author B.B.C. Radio, 19 March 1965; E15, E15A.

'Ring, The': *Irish Statesman*, 28 July 1928.

'Rising, The' (= 'Eternal Triangle' = 'The Tram'): *Cornhill Magazine*, Autumn 1951.

'Rivals, The' (= 'Judas', *see above*): *New Yorker*, 26 October 1946; B.B.C. Radio, 14 March 1947.

'Romantic, A': *Evening News*, August 1951; E2, E9.

'Ryan Woman, That' (= 'Ugly Duckling', *see below*): *Saturday Evening Post*, 19 January 1957.

'Saint, The': *Mademoiselle*, June 1952; *Housewife*, July 1953; E15, E15A.

'Salesman's Romance, A': *New Yorker*, 3 March 1956; *John Bull*, 2 February 1957; Radio Eireann, 23 May 1959; C.B.C., May 1966; E11, E12, G3; trans. German 'Abenteuer eines Handelsreisenden', also Danish, Dutch and French.

'School for Wives, The': *New Yorker*, 5 November 1966; E15, E15A.

'Sense of Responsibility, A': *New Yorker*, 2 August 1952; E9, E13.

'Sentry, The': *Harper's Bazaar*, January 1950; read by author B.B.C. Radio, 15 May 1951; E7, E9, E13, E17, G1; trans. German 'So sind sie, die Engländer'.

'September Dawn': *Dublin Magazine*, July 1929; E1.

'Set of Variations on a Borrowed Theme, A' (='Variations on a Theme'): *New Yorker*, 30 April 1960; E15, E15A; *Winter's Tales*, 11 (1965).

'Shepherds, The' (= 'The Star that bids the shepherds fold' = 'And we in herds Thy game'): E9, G4; trans. German 'Die Hirten'.

'Sinner, The': *Argosy*, March 1946.

'Sion': *Irish Tribune*, 6 August 1926.

'Sissy, The' (= 'The Genius', *see above*).

'Sisters, The': E1.

'Soirée chez une jeune belle fille': E1.

'Soldiers are We' (= 'Jo'): *Irish Statesman*, 8 March 1930.

'Solo on Gabriel's Trumpet': *Irish Times*, 28 March 1942.

'Song without Words': *Harper's Bazaar*, February 1944; *Lilliput*, May 1944; read by author B.B.C. Radio, 27 October 1942 and 2 September 1943; E4, E8, E10, E12, E14, D1; trans. Danish 'Sang uden Ord', also Italian.

'Sorcerer's Apprentice, The' (= 'Don Juan's Apprentice', *see above*): *Harper's Bazaar*, August 1954; E9, E13, G9; trans. German 'Der Zauberlehrling'.

'Spring Day, A' (= 'Baptismal'): *Reginald Moore's Modern Reading*, February 1952.

'Star that bids the shepherds fold, The' (= 'And we in herds thy game' = 'The Shepherds'): E4, E13.

'Stepmother, The': *Irish Writing no. 1* (1946); E6; trans. German 'Die Stiefmutter'.

'Story by Maupassant, A': *Penguin New Writing no. 24* (1945); E15, E15A; *Winter's Tales*, 14 (1968).

'Storyteller, The': *Harper's Bazaar*, 1937, *Best British Short Stories* (1938); trans. German, 'Wenn der Tod kommt'.

'Study of History, The': *New Yorker*, 9 March 1957; E11, E12, E14, G4; trans. German 'Mein Studium der Vergangenheit'.

'Sue': *New Yorker*, 27 September 1958; E15, E15A.

'Teacher's Mass, The': *New Yorker*, 30 April 1955; E15, E15A.

'Tears, Idle Tears': E2.

'There is a Lone House': *Golden Book*, no. 7, January 1933.

'Thief, The' (= 'Christmas Morning', *see above*); E7.

'Thing of Nothing, A': *Cornhill Magazine*, April 1946; E6, G4; trans. German 'Ein Kleinigkeit'.

'Tinker, The': B.B.C. Radio, 17 March 1943.

'Torrent Dammed, A': *New Yorker*, 3 September 1952; E9; *Pick of Today's Short Stories*, 1 (1954).

'Tram, The' (= 'Eternal Triangle' = 'The Rising'): *Atlantic Monthly*, October 1954.

'Twilight': *Lovat Dickson's Magazine*.

'Ugly Duckling, The' (= 'That Ryan Woman', *see above*): E11, E12, G4; *Saturday Evening Post Stories*, 1957; *The Irish Genius* (New York 1959); trans. German 'Das hässliche Entlein'.

'Unapproved Route': *New Yorker*, 27 September 1952; E9, E15.

'Uprooted': *Criterion*, January 1937; *The Bell*, December 1942; E4, E5, E8, E10, E12, G2; *Best British Short Stories* (1937); *Ten Modern Masters* (New York 1953, 1959, 1960); trans. German 'Entwurzelt'.

'Vanity': *New Yorker*, 18 July 1953; E9, E13.

'Variations on a Theme' (= 'Set of Variations on a Borrowed Theme'): *Winter's Tales*, 11 (1965); E15.

'War': *Irish Statesman*, 7 August 1926.

'Weeping Children, The': *New Yorker*, 21 January 1961; E13, E15A, G5; trans. German 'Die weinenden Kinder'.

'What Girls are for': *Colliers*, 17 March 1951; *John Bull*, 14 July 1951.

'What's wrong with the country': E2.

'Wild Lomasneys, The' (= 'The Mad Lomasneys'): *The Bell*, October 1942.

'World of Art and Reilly': *Vogue*, July 1948; read by author B.B.C. Radio, 6 August 1951.

'Wreath, The': *Atlantic Monthly*, November 1955; *Kilkenny Magazine*, Summer 1962; E13, E15A; trans. German 'Der Kranz'.

ABOUT FRANK O'CONNOR

'Mr Frank O'Connor' (H. A. Bruce), in *Our Heritage and other addresses* (Macmillan 1934), 384.

'The Poetry of Frank O'Connor' (Geoffrey Taylor), in *The Bell*, December 1945.

Biographical Note, in *Irish Writing*, no. 1 (1946), 115.

'Coloured Balloons – a study of Frank O'Connor' (Patrick Kavanagh), in *The Bell*, 3 December 1947.

'Frank O'Connor's Art' (F. Hackett), in *On Judging Books in General and in Particular* (Day, New York 1947), 244.

'Meet Frank O'Connor' (Bellman), in *The Bell*, 6 March 1951.

'Portrait of Frank O'Connor', in *Time*, 25 December 1944.

'A Portrait of Frank O'Connor', in *Saturday Review of Literature*, 30 October 1954.

'About the Irish', in *Nation*, 4 December 1954.

'Novel's Course' (J. Finn), in *Commonweal*, 26 October 1955.

'O'Connor's "Uprooted"' (H. E. Gerber), in *Explicator*, October 1955.

'Author of the Week' (T. E. Cooney), in *Saturday Review of Literature*, 22 September 1956.

'Frank O'Connor' (H. Breit), in *The Writer Observed* (World Publishing Co. 1956).

'Symbolism and the Student' (W. Havighurst), in *College English*, XVI (1955).

'A Portrait of Frank O'Connor', in *Saturday Review of Literature*, 21 September 1957.

'Frank O'Connor' (A. Whittier), in *The Paris Review Interviews* (Viking Press 1958).

'Frank O'Connor as Paradigm (D. Weiss), in *North West Review*, Spring 1959.

'This Side of Innisfree', in *Reporter*, 22 December 1960.

'Hurt of the Irish' (P. O'Donovan), in *New Republic*, 13 March 1961.

'Irish Poetry and Life', in *Times Literary Supplement*, 30 June 1961.

'Artist as a Boy', in *Newsweek*, 13 March 1961.

'The O'Connors of Cork' (Vivian Mercier), in *New York Times Book Review*, 12 March 1961.

'A Personal Memoir in a great Tradition' (W. T. Scott), in *Herald Tribune*, 12 March 1961.

'Frank O'Connor and Goethe' (J. Hennig), in *Neue Folge des Jahrbuchs den Goethe Weimar*, XXIV (1962).

'A Storyteller and his Craft' (Frank MacManus), in *RTE Guide*, 9 February 1962.

'Masters of Instant Truth' (W. Bower), in *Saturday Review of Literature*, 20 July 1963.

'For Decency Sake' (P. Lennon), in *Manchester Guardian*, 9 October 1963.

'Translations of Frank O'Connor' (Douglas Sealy), in *Dubliner*, Summer 1963.

'Frank O'Connor' (Elisabeth Schnack), in *Neue Zürcher Zeitung*, 9 September 1964.

'O'Connor's Unflattering Picture of Bourgeois Ireland' (Bernard Share), in *Hibernia*, January 1965.

'A Consideration of Frank O'Connor's Short Stories' (George B. Saul), in *Colby Library Quarterly*, December 1963.

Notes on the Contributors

DEBORAH AVERILL, M.A., was born in Poughkeepsie, New York, in 1943. She studied Anglo-Irish literature at Trinity College, Dublin, under Frank O'Connor, and has recently completed her Ph.D. thesis on his short stories.

DANIEL A. BINCHY, M.A., D.PHIL., was born in Charleville, County Cork, in 1900. He was educated at University College, Dublin, and in Berlin, Munich and Paris. He was Irish Ambassador to Germany from 1929 to 1932 and then became professor of Jurisprudence, Roman Law and Legal History at University College, Dublin. He was Senior Research Fellow at Corpus Christi College, Oxford, from 1946 to 1950. He has published *Church and State in Fascist Italy* and a large number of articles on Old Irish and Early Irish history; and in 1963 the definitive work on St Patrick and beginnings of Christianity in Ireland, 'St Patrick and his biographers, old and new'. He met Frank O'Connor in 1927. At present he is Senior Professor at the Dublin Institute for Advanced Studies.

EAVAN BOLAND was born in Dublin in 1944. She was educated in Trinity College, Dublin, and in London and New York. She has published three books of poetry and has contributed poems and articles to Irish journals. In 1967 she became lecturer in English literature at Trinity College. In 1968 she received the Macaulay Fellowship for Poetry.

DONAL BRENNAN was born in Clooncraff, County Roscommon, in 1919. He served in the Intelligence Corps of the Irish Army during World War II and subsequently became manager of the national airline, Aer Lingus, in France. He has written articles on French and Irish literature for Irish and British newspapers. He met Frank O'Connor in 1956 and travelled widely with him in France.

PHILIP EDWARDS, M.A., PH.D., was born in Lancashire, England, in 1923. He was educated at Birmingham University and subsequently served in the Royal Navy during World War II. He lectured in the Department of English at Birmingham University from 1946 and became Commonwealth Fellow at Harvard in 1954-5. He was Professor of English at Trinity College, Dublin, from 1960 to 1966. He met Frank O'Connor in 1963. Among his books are *Sir Walter Ralegh*, *The Spanish Tragedy*, *Thomas Kyd and Early Elizabethan Tragedy* and *Shakespeare and the Confines of Art*. At present he is Professor of Literature at the University of Essex.

RICHARD ELLMANN, M.A., PH.D., was born in 1918 at Highland Park, Michigan. He was educated at Yale University and Trinity College, Dublin. In 1951 he became Professor of English at Northwestern University. Among his books are *Yeats, the Man and the Masks*, *James Joyce* and *The Identity of Yeats*. He met Frank O'Connor in Dublin in 1947. At present he is Professor of English at Yale University.

THOMAS FLANAGAN, M.A., PH.D., was born in Greenwich, Connecticut, in 1923. He was educated at Amherst College and Columbia University. He is author of *The Irish Novelists, 1800–1850* and of essays and articles in *The Kenyon Review, Ramparts, Victorian Studies* and other periodicals. He met Frank O'Connor in 1960 when he studied there as a Guggenheim Fellow. At present he is Associate Professor of English at the University of California in Berkeley.

DERMOT FOLEY was born in Dublin in 1908. He began his career as Librarian under Frank O'Connor at Pembroke Library in Dublin. Subsequently he was Librarian for Clare County and Cork City. At present he is the Director of the Library Council of Ireland.

RICHARD T. GILL, PH.D., was born in Long Beach, New Jersey, in 1927. He was educated at Harvard and became Assistant Dean there from 1949 to 1952. He met Frank O'Connor in 1953, when he acted as assistant to Frank O'Connor's writing course at Harvard. In 1954 he won the Atlantic First Short Story Prize. His short stories have been published in the *New Yorker* and the *Atlantic Monthly*. He became lecturer in economics at Harvard in 1963. At present he is Master of Leverett House.

DAVID GREENE, M.A., was born in Dublin in 1915. He was educated at Trinity College, Dublin and became lecturer in Celtic there in 1938. He was Professor at the Dublin Institute for Advanced Studies from

1948 to 1955, when he became Professor of Irish at Trinity College. He published *Fingal Róndin and other Stories* in 1955 and was co-author with Frank O'Connor of *A Golden Treasury of Irish Poetry, A.D. 600 to 1200* in 1967. He has also contributed to scholarly journals on Old Irish. At present he is Senior Professor at the Dublin Institute for Advanced Studies.

SEAN HENDRICK was born in Cork in April 1900. He first met Frank O'Connor in 1920, when they were both members of A Company, 1st Cork Brigade of the I.R.A. After the Civil War he contributed articles to the *Irish Statesman* and other journals. At the same period he was co-founder with Frank O'Connor of the Cork Drama League. He has since been a leading member of the cultural life of Cork, a council member of the Cork International Film Festival, secretary of the Cork Advisory Body of the Arts Council and member of the Cork Sculpture Committee.

BRENDAN KENNELLY, M.A., PH.D., was born in Ballylongford, County Kerry in 1936. He studied at Trinity College, Dublin, and Leeds University. He has published three books of poetry and two novels. In 1967 he won the AE award for poetry. He worked with Frank O'Connor on the B.B.C. film concerning W. B. Yeats, 'Horseman Pass By', and as an assistant in Trinity College. At present he is attached to the Department of English at Trinity College.

SHEVAWN LYNAM was born in Dublin and educated in Ireland, England, France and Spain. Her early career was spent working at film scripts for Alfred Hitchcock and Robert Donat, after which she spent the war years in the Ministry of Information in Dublin and London. She spent thirteen years in Paris as a press relations officer for the Marshall Plan, UNESCO, the British Embassy and finally NATO. Her first short story 'Back to Gurthreevagh' appeared in 1955, and her other writing includes the novel *The Spirit and the Clay*. She met Frank O'Connor in 1940. At present she is editorial publicity officer with the Irish Tourist Board.

ROGER MCHUGH, M.A., PH.D., was born in Dublin in 1908. He was educated in University College, Dublin and later joined the staff of the Department of English there. He has lectured in the United States, Russia and Scandinavia. For his plays he was awarded the Abbey Theatre Prize in 1945 and the Pitre Prize in 1958. His other works include a biography of Henry Grattan and editions of the letters of W. B.

Yeats and of the autobiography of Maud Gonne MacBride. He is trustee of the Lyric Players Theatre, Belfast. At present he is Professor of Anglo-Irish Literature and Drama at University College, Dublin.

WILLIAM MAXWELL was born in 1908 at Lincoln, Illinois. He was educated at the University of Illinois and became a member of the staff of the Department of English there in 1931. He has written five novels, among them *They Came Like Swallows*, one children's book *The Heavenly Twins* and a book of tales *The Old Man at the Railroad Crossing*. He has also written numerous short stories. He became editor at the *New Yorker* magazine in 1936 and met Frank O'Connor in 1954.

MAURICE SHEEHY, PH.D., D.LITT., was born in Dublin in 1928. He was educated at University College, Dublin, and in France and Italy. He has published a source-book for the middle ages, *Pontificia Hibernica: Medieval Papal Documents concerning Ireland, 640–1261* and articles concerning early and medieval history. In 1963 he was awarded the Irish Historical Research Prize of the National University. He met Frank O'Connor in 1963, and since the author's death has edited the unfinished autobiography *My Father's Son*. At present he is attached to the Department of Palaeography and Late Latin at University College, Dublin.

WALLACE STEGNER, M.A., PH.D., was born in Lake Mills, Iowa, in 1909. He was educated at the University of Iowa and taught English at Harvard from 1934 to 1944. He became Professor of English and Director of the Creative Writing Centre at Stanford University in 1945. He has published novels, among them *Big Rock Candy Mountain* and the most recent, *All the Little Live Things*; and books of short stories, and topographical historical books, including *Mormon Country* and *Wolf Willow*. He met Frank O'Connor at Stanford in 1956.

HONOR TRACY was born in England in 1913. She was educated in London and in Germany and France. During World War II she worked with the Ministry of Information in London. She began her writing career after the war, when she moved to Ireland and became involved with *The Bell*. She has written short stories and articles for English and American journals. Her non-fiction works include books on Japan, Ireland and Spain. Her novels include *The Straight and Narrow Path*, *The Prospects are Pleasing*, *A Number of Things*, *Men at Work* and *The Beauty of the World*. At present she lives in Achill island in the west of Ireland.